JAMESTOWN EDUCATION

Timed Readings Plus

in Social Studies

BOOK 2

**25 Two-Part Lessons with Questions for
Building Reading Speed and Comprehension**

Mc
Graw
Hill **Glencoe**

New York, New York Columbus, Ohio Chicago, Illinois Peoria, Illinois Woodland Hills, California

JAMESTOWN EDUCATION

Glencoe

The *McGraw·Hill* Companies

ISBN: 0-07-845800-5

Send all queries to:
Glencoe/McGraw-Hill
8787 Orion Place
Columbus, OH 43240-4027

1 2 3 4 5 6 7 8 9 10   021   08 07 06 05 04 03

CONTENTS

You probably talk at an average rate of about 150 words a minute. If you are a reader of average ability, you read at a rate of about 250 words a minute. So your reading speed is nearly twice as fast as your speaking or listening speed. This example shows that reading is one of the fastest ways to get information.

The purpose of this book is to help you increase your reading rate and understand what you read. The 25 lessons in this book will also give you practice in reading social studies articles and in preparing for tests in which you must read and understand nonfiction passages within a certain time limit.

Reading Faster and Better

Following are some strategies that you can use to read the articles in each lesson.

Previewing

Previewing before you read is a very important step. This helps you to get an idea of what a selection is about and to recall any previous knowledge you have about the subject. Here are the steps to follow when previewing.

Read the title. Titles are designed not only to announce the subject but also to make the reader think. Ask yourself questions such as What can I learn from the title? What thoughts does it bring to mind?

What do I already know about this subject?

Read the first sentence. If they are short, read the first two sentences. The opening sentence is the writer's opportunity to get your attention. Some writers announce what they hope to tell you in the selection. Some writers state their purpose for writing; others just try to get your attention.

Read the last sentence. If it is short, read the final two sentences. The closing sentence is the writer's last chance to get ideas across to you. Some writers repeat the main idea once more. Some writers draw a conclusion—this is what they have been leading up to. Other writers summarize their thoughts; they tie all the facts together.

Skim the entire selection. Glance through the selection quickly to see what other information you can pick up. Look for anything that will help you read fluently and with understanding. Are there names, dates, or numbers? If so, you may have to read more slowly.

Reading for Meaning

Here are some ways to make sure you are making sense of what you read.

Build your concentration. You cannot understand what you read if you are not concentrating. When you discover that your thoughts are straying, correct the situation right away. Avoid distractions and distracting situations. Keep in mind the information you learned from previewing. This will help focus your attention on the selection.

Read in thought groups. Try to see meaningful combinations of words—phrases, clauses, or sentences. If you look at only one word at a time (called word-by-word reading), both your comprehension and your reading speed suffer.

Ask yourself questions. To sustain the pace you have set for yourself and to maintain a high level of concentration and comprehension, ask yourself questions such as What does this mean? or How can I use this information? as you read.

Finding the Main Ideas

The paragraph is the basic unit of meaning. If you can quickly discover and understand the main idea of each paragraph, you will build your comprehension of the selection.

Find the topic sentence. The topic sentence, which contains the main idea, often is the first sentence of a paragraph. It is followed by sentences that support, develop, or explain the main idea. Sometimes a topic sentence comes at the end of a paragraph. When it does, the supporting details come first, building the base for the topic sentence. Some paragraphs do not have a topic sentence; all of the sentences combine to create a meaningful idea.

Understand paragraph structure. Every well-written paragraph has a purpose. The purpose may be to inform, define, explain, or illustrate. The purpose should always relate to the main idea and expand on it. As you read each paragraph, see how the body of the paragraph tells you more about the main idea.

Relate ideas as you read. As you read the selection, notice how the writer puts together ideas. As you discover the relationship between the ideas, the main ideas come through quickly and clearly.

Mastering Reading Comprehension

Reading fast is not useful if you don't remember or understand what you read. The two exercises in Part A provide a check on how well you have understood the article.

Recalling Facts

These multiple-choice questions provide a quick check to see how well you recall important information from the article. As you learn to apply the reading strategies described earlier, you should be able to answer these questions more successfully.

Understanding Ideas

These questions require you to think about the main ideas in the article. Some main ideas are stated in the article; others are not. To answer some of the questions, you need to draw conclusions about what you read.

The five exercises in Part B require multiple answers. These exercises provide practice in applying comprehension and critical thinking skills that you can use in all your reading.

Recognizing Words in Context

Always check to see whether the words around an unfamiliar word—its context—can give you a clue to the word's meaning. A word generally appears in a context related to its meaning.

Suppose, for example, that you are unsure of the meaning of the word *expired* in the following passage:

> Vera wanted to check out a book, but her library card had expired. She had to borrow my card, because she didn't have time to renew hers.

You could begin to figure out the meaning of *expired* by asking yourself a question such as, What could have happened to Vera's library card that would make her need to borrow someone else's card? You might realize that if Vera had to renew her card, its usefulness must have come to an end or run out. This would lead you to conclude that the word *expired* must mean "to come to an end" or "to run out." You would be right. The context suggested the meaning.

Context can also affect the meaning of a word you already know. The word *key,* for instance, has many meanings. There are musical keys, door keys, and keys to solving a mystery. The context in which the word *key* occurs will tell you which meaning is correct.

Sometimes a word is explained by the words that immediately follow it. The subject of a sentence and your knowledge about that subject might also help you determine the meaning of an unknown word. Try to decide the meaning of the word *revive* in the following sentence:

> Sunshine and water will revive those drooping plants.

The compound subject is *sunshine* and *water.* You know that plants need light and water to survive and that drooping plants are not healthy. You can figure out that *revive* means "to bring back to health."

Distinguishing Fact from Opinion

Every day you are called upon to sort out fact and opinion. Because much of what you read and hear contains both facts and opinions, you need to be able to tell the two apart.

Facts are statements that can be proved. The proof must be objective and verifiable. You must be able to check for yourself to confirm a fact.

Look at the following facts. Notice that they can be checked for accuracy and confirmed. Suggested sources for verification appear in parentheses.

- Abraham Lincoln was the 16th president of the United States. (Consult biographies, social studies books, encyclopedias, and similar sources.)

- Earth revolves around the Sun. (Research in encyclopedias or astronomy books; ask knowledgeable people.)

- Dogs walk on four legs. (See for yourself.)

Opinions are statements that cannot be proved. There is no objective evidence you can consult to check the truthfulness of an opinion. Unlike facts, opinions express personal beliefs or judgments. Opinions reveal how someone feels about a subject, not the facts about that subject. You might agree or disagree with someone's opinion, but you cannot prove it right or wrong.

Look at the following opinions. The reasons these statements are classified as opinions appear in parentheses.

- Abraham Lincoln was born to be a president. (You cannot prove this by referring to birth records. There is no evidence to support this belief.)

- Earth is the only planet in our solar system where intelligent life exists. (There is no proof of this. It may be proved true some day, but for now it is just an educated guess—not a fact.)

- The dog is a human's best friend. (This is not a fact; your best friend might not be a dog.)

As you read, be aware that facts and opinions are often mixed together. Both are useful to you as a reader. But to evaluate what you read and to read intelligently, you need to know the difference between the two.

Keeping Events in Order

Sequence, or chronological order, is the order of events in a story or article or the order of steps in a process. Paying attention to the sequence of events or steps will help you follow what is happening, predict what might happen next, and make sense of a passage.

To make the sequence as clear as possible, writers often use signal words to help the reader get a more exact idea of when things happen. Following is a list of frequently used signal words and phrases:

until	first
next	then
before	after
finally	later
when	while
during	now
at the end	by the time
as soon as	in the beginning

Signal words and phrases are also useful when a writer chooses to relate details or events out of sequence. You need to pay careful attention to determine the correct chronological order.

Making Correct Inferences

Much of what you read *suggests* more than it *says*. Writers often do not state ideas directly in a text. They can't. Think of the time and space it would take to state every idea. And think of how boring that would be! Instead, writers leave it to you, the reader, to fill in the information they leave out—to make inferences. You do this by combining clues in the story or article with knowledge from your own experience.

You make many inferences every day. Suppose, for example, that you are visiting a friend's house for the first time. You see a bag of kitty litter. You infer (make an inference) that the family has a cat. Another day you overhear a conversation. You catch the names of two actors and the words *scene, dialogue,* and *directing*. You infer that the people are discussing a movie or play.

In these situations and others like them, you infer unstated information from what you observe or read. Readers must make inferences in order to understand text.

Be careful about the inferences you make. One set of facts may suggest several inferences. Some of these inferences could be faulty. A correct inference must be supported by evidence.

Remember that bag of kitty litter that caused you to infer that your friend has a cat? That could be a faulty inference. Perhaps your friend's family uses the kitty litter on their icy sidewalks to create traction. To be sure your inference is correct, you need more evidence.

Understanding Main Ideas

The main idea is the most important idea in a paragraph or passage—the idea that provides purpose and direction. The rest of the selection explains, develops, or supports the main idea. Without a main idea, there would be only a collection of unconnected thoughts.

In the following paragraph, the main idea is printed in italics. As you read, observe how the other sentences develop or explain the main idea.

Typhoon Chris hit with full fury today on the central coast of Japan. Heavy rain from the storm flooded the area. High waves carried many homes into the sea. People now fear that the heavy rains will cause mudslides in the central part of the country. The number of people killed by the storm may climb past the 200 mark by Saturday.

In this paragraph, the main-idea statement appears first. It is followed by sentences that explain, support, or give details. Sometimes the main idea appears at the end of a paragraph. Writers often put the main idea at the end of a paragraph when their purpose is to persuade or convince. Readers may be more open to a new idea if the reasons for it are presented first.

As you read the following paragraph, think about the overall impact of the supporting ideas. Their purpose is to convince the reader that the main idea in the last sentence should be accepted.

Last week there was a head-on collision at Huntington and Canton streets. Just a month ago a pedestrian was struck there. Fortunately, she was only slightly injured. In the past year, there have been more accidents there than at any other corner in the city. In fact, nearly 10 percent of all accidents in the city occur at the corner. This intersection is very dangerous, and a traffic signal should be installed there before a life is lost.

The details in the paragraph progress from least important to most important. They achieve their full effect in the main idea statement at the end.

In many cases, the main idea is not expressed in a single sentence. The reader is called upon to interpret all of the ideas expressed in the paragraph and to decide upon a main idea. Read the following paragraph.

> The American author Jack London was once a pupil at the Cole Grammar School in Oakland, California. Each morning the class sang a song. When the teacher noticed that Jack wouldn't sing, she sent him to the principal. He returned to class with a note. The note said that Jack could be excused from singing with the class if he would write an essay every morning.

In this paragraph, the reader has to interpret the individual ideas and to decide on a main idea. This main idea seems reasonable: Jack London's career as a writer began with a punishment in grammar school.

Understanding the concept of the main idea and knowing how to find it is important. Transferring that understanding to your reading and study is also important.

Working Through a Lesson

Part A

1. **Preview the article.** Locate the timed selection in Part A of the lesson that you are going to read. Wait for your teacher's signal to preview. You will have 20 seconds for previewing. Follow the previewing steps described on page 2.

2. **Read the article.** When your teacher gives you the signal, begin reading. Read carefully so that you will be able to answer questions about what you have read. When you finish reading, look at the board and note your reading time. Write this time at the bottom of the page on the line labeled Reading Time.

3. **Complete the exercises.** Answer the 10 questions that follow the article. There are 5 fact questions and 5 idea questions. Choose the best answer to each question and put an X in that box.

4. **Correct your work.** Use the Answer Key at the back of the book to check your answers. Circle any wrong answer and put an X in the box you should have marked. Record the number of correct answers on the appropriate line at the end of the lesson.

Part B

1. **Preview and read the passage.** Use the same techniques you

used to read Part A. Think about what you are reading.

2. **Complete the exercises.** Instructions are given for answering each category of question. There are 15 responses for you to record.

3. **Correct your work.** Use the Answer Key at the back of the book. Circle any wrong answer and write the correct letter or number next to it. Record the number of correct answers on the appropriate line at the end of the lesson.

Plotting Your Progress

1. **Find your reading rate.** Turn to the Reading Rate graph on page 116. Put an X at the point where the vertical line that represents the lesson intersects your reading time, shown along the left-hand side. The right-hand side of the graph will reveal your words-per-minute reading speed.

2. **Find your comprehension score.** Add your scores for Part A and Part B to determine your total number of correct answers. Turn to the Comprehension Score Graph on page 117. Put an X at the point where the vertical line that represents your lesson intersects your total correct answers, shown along the left-hand side. The right-hand side of the graph will show the percentage of questions you answered correctly.

3. **Complete the Comprehension Skills Profile.** Turn to page 118. Record your incorrect answers for the Part B exercises. The five Part B skills are listed along the bottom. There are five columns of boxes, one column for each question. For every incorrect answer, put an X in a box for that skill.

To get the most benefit from these lessons, you need to take charge of your own progress in improving your reading speed and comprehension. Studying these graphs will help you to see whether your reading rate is increasing and to determine what skills you need to work on. Your teacher will also review the graphs to check your progress.

TO THE TEACHER

About the Series

Timed Readings Plus in Social Studies includes 10 books at reading levels 4–13, with one book at each level. Book One contains material at a fourth-grade reading level; Book Two at a fifth-grade level, and so on. The readability level is determined by the Fry Readability Scale and is not to be confused with grade or age level of the student. The books are designed for use with students at middle school level and above.

The purposes of the series are as follows:

- to provide systematic, structured reading practice that helps students improve their reading rate and comprehension skills

- to give students practice in reading and understanding informational articles in the content area of social studies

- to give students experience in reading various text types—informational, expository, narrative, and prescriptive

- to prepare students for taking standardized tests that include timed reading passages in various content areas

- to provide materials with a wide range of reading levels so that students can continue to practice and improve their reading rate and comprehension skills

Because the books are designed for use with students at designated reading levels rather than in a particular grade, the social studies topics in this series are not correlated to any grade-level curriculum. Most standardized tests require students to read and comprehend social studies passages. This series provides an opportunity for students to become familiar with the particular requirements of reading social studies. For example, the vocabulary in a social studies article is important. Students need to know certain words in order to understand the concepts and the information.

Each book in the series contains 25 two-part lessons. Part A focuses on improving reading rate. This section of the lesson consists of a 400-word timed informational article on a social studies topic followed by two multiple-choice exercises. Recalling Facts includes five fact questions; Understanding Ideas includes five critical thinking questions.

Part B concentrates on building mastery in critical areas of comprehension. This section consists of a nontimed passage—the "plus" passage—followed by five exercises that address five major comprehension skills. The passage varies in length; its subject matter relates to the content of the timed selection.

Timed Reading and Comprehension

Timed reading is the best-known method of improving reading speed. There is no point in someone's reading at an accelerated speed if the person does not understand what she or he is reading. Nothing is more important than comprehension in reading. The main purpose of reading is to gain knowledge and insight, to understand the information that the writer and the text are communicating.

Few students will be able to read a passage once and answer all of the questions correctly. A score of 70 or 80 percent correct is normal. If the student gets 90 or 100 percent correct, he or she is either reading too slowly or the material is at too low a reading level. A comprehension or critical thinking score of less than 70 percent indicates a need for improvement.

One method of improving comprehension and critical thinking skills is for the student to go back and study each incorrect answer. First, the student should reread the question carefully. It is surprising how many students get the wrong answer simply because they have not read the question carefully. Then the student should look back in the passage to find the place where the question is answered, reread that part of the passage, and think about how to arrive at the correct answer. It is important to be able to recognize a correct answer when it is embedded in the text. Teacher guidance or class discussion will help the student find an answer.

Speed Versus Comprehension

It is not unusual for comprehension scores to decline as reading rate increases during the early weeks of timed readings. If this happens, students should attempt to level off their speed—but not lower it—and concentrate more on comprehension. Usually, if students maintain the higher speed and concentrate on comprehension, scores will gradually improve and within a week or two be back up to normal levels of 70 to 80 percent.

It is important to achieve a proper balance between speed and comprehension. An inefficient reader typically reads everything at one speed, usually slowly. Some poor readers, however, read rapidly but without satisfactory comprehension. It is important to achieve a balance between speed and comprehension. The practice that this series provides enables students to increase their reading speed while maintaining normal levels of comprehension.

Getting Started

As a rule, the passages in a book designed to improve reading speed should be relatively easy. The student should not have much difficulty with the vocabulary or the subject matter. Don't worry about the passages being too easy; students should see how quickly and efficiently they can read a passage.

Begin by assigning students to a level. A student should start with a book that is one level below his or her current reading level. If a student's reading level is not known, a suitable starting point would be one or two levels below the student's present grade in school.

Introduce students to the contents and format of the book they are using. Examine the book to see how it is organized. Talk about the parts of each lesson. Discuss the purpose of timed reading and the use of the progress graphs at the back of the book.

Timing the Reading

One suggestion for timing the reading is to have all students begin reading the selection at the same time. After one minute, write on the board the time that has elapsed and begin updating it at 10-second intervals (1:00, 1:10, 1:20, etc.). Another option is to have individual students time themselves with a stopwatch.

Teaching a Lesson

Part A

1. Give students the signal to begin previewing the lesson. Allow 20 seconds, then discuss special terms or vocabulary that students found.

2. Use one of the methods described above to time students as they read the passage. (Include the 20-second preview time as part of the first minute.) Tell students to write down the last time shown on the board or the stopwatch when they finish reading. Have them record the time in the designated space after the passage.

3. Next, have students complete the exercises in Part A. Work with them to check their answers, using the Answer Key that begins on page 114. Have them circle incorrect answers, mark the correct answers, and then record the numbers of correct answers for Part A on the appropriate line at the end of the lesson. Correct responses to eight or more questions indicate satisfactory comprehension and recall.

Part B

1. Have students read the Part B passage and complete the exercises that follow it. Directions are provided with each exercise. Correct responses require deliberation and discrimination.

2. Work with students to check their answers. Then discuss the answers with them and have them record the number of correct answers for Part B at the end of the lesson.

Have students study the correct answers to the questions they answered incorrectly. It is important that they understand why a particular answer is correct or incorrect.

Have them reread relevant parts of a passage to clarify an answer. An effective cooperative activity is to have students work in pairs to discuss their answers, explain why they chose the answers they did, and try to resolve differences.

Monitoring Progress

Have students find their total correct answers for the lesson and record their reading time and scores on the graphs on pages 116 and 117. Then have them complete the Comprehension Skills Profile on page 118. For each incorrect response to a question in Part B, students should mark an X in the box above each question type.

The legend on the Reading Rate graph automatically converts reading times to words-per-minute rates. The Comprehension Score graph automatically converts the raw scores to percentages.

These graphs provide a visual record of a student's progress. This record gives the student and you an opportunity to evaluate the student's progress and to determine the types of exercises and skills he or she needs to concentrate on.

Diagnosis and Evaluation

The following are typical reading rates.

Slow Reader—150 Words Per Minute

Average Reader—250 Words Per Minute

Fast Reader—350 Words Per Minute

A student who consistently reads at an average or above-average rate (with satisfactory comprehension) is ready to advance to the next book in the series.

A column of Xs in the Comprehension Skills Profile indicates a specific comprehension weakness. Using the profile, you can assess trends in student performance and suggest remedial work if necessary.

Birthday Traditions Around the World

People in different parts of the world have different birthday traditions. In the United States, people often celebrate a birthday at a party. They give presents and serve cake and ice cream. But in Korea people celebrate by eating seaweed soup and rice cakes. Koreans serve seaweed soup, because it is healthful, and special rice cakes decorated with nuts and dried fruit. Traditional dress, called *hanbok*, may be worn. The jacket is made like a blouse with long sleeves. Women wear skirts, and men wear baggy pants.

In China people eat "longevity noodles" on their birthdays. These long noodles symbolize long life. Children do not have birthday parties because parents do not want the gods to notice them until they are grown up. On a child's birthday, special foods may be served that include an egg dish. The child is urged to eat the yolk. In Chinese, the word for "yolk" sounds the same as the word for "control." Eating the yolk reminds children that the adults guide them. Parents give their children money in a red envelope for luck. Adults have birthday parties, and the sixtieth birthday is a big celebration.

Children in Mexico have birthday parties with family and friends. A hollow figure in the shape of an animal, flower, or favorite thing is filled with candy and prizes. It is called a piñata, and it is hung from the ceiling. The children, who are blindfolded, take turns striking the piñata with a stick. The child who breaks it will have good luck. When the piñata breaks, everyone grabs the treasures that fall out.

A *kinderfest* is a child's birthday party in Germany. Historians think the Germans were the first to have birthday parties for children. A wooden birthday wreath with candles on it is placed on the table. A tall candle in the middle, the "life" candle, is lit every year until a child becomes 12 years old. The food is homemade by the mother, who cooks all day to prepare for this event.

A child at a birthday party in Canada may find a coin in the cake. The child who finds it goes first when party games are played. Guests may be given "crackers." A cracker is a tube decorated in colored paper. A paper strip is used to pull the cracker apart. It makes a loud bang. Inside may be a prize or a paper that tells the person's fortune.

Reading Time _____

Recalling Facts

1. The Korean traditional dress is called a
   - ❑ a. piñata
   - ❑ b. hanbok
   - ❑ c. kinderfest.

2. People eat longevity noodles on their birthdays in
   - ❑ a. China.
   - ❑ b. Mexico.
   - ❑ c. Germany.

3. In China children are given _____ on their birthdays.
   - ❑ a. a wooden birthday wreath
   - ❑ b. money in a red envelope for luck
   - ❑ c. crackers

4. In Germany, on a child's birthday, people light a
   - ❑ a. "life" candle.
   - ❑ b. firecracker.
   - ❑ c. piñata.

5. In Canada a "cracker" is a
   - ❑ a. red envelope.
   - ❑ b. very long noodle.
   - ❑ c. tube decorated in colored paper that makes a loud bang.

Understanding Ideas

6. Which of the following sentences tells what the whole passage is about?
   - ❑ a. Historians think that the Germans were the first to have birthday parties for children.
   - ❑ b. People around the world honor the life of a person in various ways on the day he or she was born.
   - ❑ c. People around the world like to celebrate for many special occasions.

7. One can infer that birthday celebrations around the world
   - ❑ a. are celebrated the same way.
   - ❑ b. reflect the different beliefs of people from different cultures.
   - ❑ c. are celebrated with cake and ice cream.

8. The person most likely to have a birthday party in China would be
   - ❑ a. a one-year-old.
   - ❑ b. a seven-year-old.
   - ❑ c. a sixty-year-old.

9. From the passage, one can conclude that a similar feature of birthdays is
   - ❑ a. a traditional dance.
   - ❑ b. special food.
   - ❑ c. colorful clothing.

10. In both Canada and China, it is most likely true that money is a symbol of
    - ❑ a. good fortune.
    - ❑ b. a long life.
    - ❑ c. a happy year.

1 B Name Days in Slovakia

My name is Igor, and today—April 10—is my name day. It is also my cousin's name day because his name is Igor, too. We live in Europe, in Slovakia. In our country, each day of the year has a name, and a person's name day is that date on the calendar that has their name. My cousin and I share our name day with all the other Igors in Slovakia.

A name day is like a second birthday but not as important. In one way, my name day is better than my birthday, because sometimes my friends forget my birthday. They never overlook my name day because it is right there on the calendar. This morning, my mother gave me a new book. My sister, Laura, gave me five flowers she grew in her garden. She gave me five flowers because an even number of flowers is considered unlucky.

At school, my cousin Igor gave me a card he had made himself. I gave him a box of his favorite chocolates. After school, my father took us both to the zoo. My sister had to stay home and do her homework. When she complained to my father, he told her that on June 5 she could go someplace that is fun, because June 5 is the name day for Laura.

1. **Recognizing Words in Context**

    Find the word *overlook* in the passage. One definition below is closest to the meaning of that word. One definition has the opposite or nearly the opposite meaning. The remaining definition has a completely different meaning. Label the definitions C for *closest*, O for *opposite or nearly opposite*, and D for *different*.

    _____ a. think

    _____ b. forget

    _____ c. remember

2. **Distinguishing Fact from Opinion**

    Two of the statements below present *facts*, which can be proved. The other statement is an *opinion*, which expresses someone's thoughts or beliefs. Label the statements F for *fact* and O for *opinion*.

    _____ a. The name day for Igor is April 10.

    _____ b. Name days should take the place of birthdays in Slovakia.

    _____ c. In Slovakia each day of the year has a name.

3. Keeping Events in Order

Number the statements below 1, 2, and 3 to show the order in which the events took place.

_____ a. After school we went to the zoo.

_____ b. This morning my mother gave me a book.

_____ c. At school Igor gave me a card.

4. Making Correct Inferences

Two of the statements below are correct *inferences,* or reasonable guesses. They are based on information in the passage. The other statement is an incorrect, or faulty, inference. Label the statements C for *correct* inference and F for *faulty* inference.

_____ a. A person's name day is celebrated by giving that person presents.

_____ b. The people of Slovakia celebrate both birthdays and name days.

_____ c. Everyone goes to the zoo on his or her name day.

5. Understanding Main Ideas

One of the statements below expresses the main idea of the passage. One statement is too general, or too broad. The other explains only part of the passage; it is too narrow. Label the statements M for *main idea*, B for *too broad*, and N for *too narrow.*

_____ a. In Slovakia people have many kinds of celebrations.

_____ b. In Slovakia people celebrate their name days, which are listed on the calendar.

_____ c. The name day for Laura is June 5.

Correct Answers, Part A _____

Correct Answers, Part B _____

Total Correct Answers _____

The 1950s Kitchen

In the 1950s, people thought cooking and cleaning were women's work. Women usually spent a great deal of time in the kitchen. Many women wanted to spend less time there. Some had jobs outside the home; others wanted more time for hobbies, school, or other interests. Inventions that saved time in the kitchen became popular.

One such device was the pop-up toaster. People had used toasters for a long time, but the bread had to be watched so that it would not burn. In 1919 a man named Charles Strite added springs and a timer to a toaster. The toast popped up when it was done. By the 1950s, pop-up toasters were used in many homes.

There were also new food ideas that saved on cooking time. Cake mixes, pudding mixes, and fast-cooking rice are a few examples. On busy days, a housewife did not have to cook at all; she could go to the freezer, take out a frozen dinner, and pop it into the oven.

Frozen dinners, also called TV dinners, were invented because the Swanson Company had too many frozen turkeys kept in refrigerated railroad cars. A man named Gerry Thomas thought the turkeys could be used in frozen dinners. He made a metal tray with three sections. This was to keep the foods in the dinner from mixing together. The first frozen dinners were sold to a vendor on the West Coast. TV dinners became very popular, and freezer sales increased.

New devices also helped make cleanup faster. The garbage disposal cut down on the waste that had to be taken out to the trash. The disposal was part of the sink. A person scraped waste off the plates into the disposal, and, with a flip of a switch, the waste was ground up and sent down the drain.

Once plates were scraped and rinsed, they could be placed in the dishwasher. Josephine Cochrane invented this device in the late 1800s. She saw that her best dishes were chipping. She thought the servants were not careful enough when they washed them. Cochrane washed her good dishes herself, but she did not like the job. She thought of a device with a rack to hold dishes while they were sprayed with water. Early dishwashers were cabinets that sat on top of the counter. At first, only hotels used them. They were not used in homes until the 1950s.

Reading Time _____

Recalling Facts

1. Charles Strite added springs and a timer to invent the
   - ❑ a. dishwasher.
   - ❑ b. garbage disposal.
   - ❑ c. pop-up toaster.

2. TV dinners were invented because
   - ❑ a. the Swanson Company had too many frozen turkeys.
   - ❑ b. consumers asked companies to sell them.
   - ❑ c. women no longer wanted to wash dishes.

3. The garbage disposal
   - ❑ a. was not used after 1960.
   - ❑ b. helped to make cleanup time faster.
   - ❑ c. led to the invention of the garbage can.

4. Josephine Cochrane invented the dishwasher because
   - ❑ a. she didn't like washing dishes by hand.
   - ❑ b. her servants refused to do the dishes by hand.
   - ❑ c. she didn't want to scrape and rinse plates.

5. The first dishwashers were used in
   - ❑ a. homes.
   - ❑ b. diners.
   - ❑ c. hotels.

Understanding Ideas

6. From reading the passage, one can conclude that in the 1950s
   - ❑ a. most women had jobs outside the home.
   - ❑ b. more women than men invented kitchen devices.
   - ❑ c. many timesaving devices for the kitchen became available.

7. Probably TV dinners were popular because
   - ❑ a. people liked turkey.
   - ❑ b. people wanted the trays the dinners came in.
   - ❑ c. they were fast and easy to prepare.

8. A pop-up toaster may save time because
   - ❑ a. the bread doesn't have to be watched.
   - ❑ b. the bread pops out of the toaster quickly.
   - ❑ c. the bread toasts at a higher heat than in a regular toaster.

9. Of the following, which would *not* help you prepare a meal faster?
   - ❑ a. dishwasher
   - ❑ b. cake mix
   - ❑ c. TV dinner

10. From reading the passage, one can conclude that inventors
    - ❑ a. most often invent things that people ask them to create.
    - ❑ b. find ways to solve problems.
    - ❑ c. are usually wealthy, so they do not need to work.

Sylvan Goldman and the Shopping Cart

One day in 1937, grocery store owner Sylvan Goldman was watching his customers shop. He thought they might buy more if they could carry more. He also thought that carrying more would make their shopping easier and more convenient. Goldman built a shopping basket that could roll. He used a folding chair for a frame and attached wheels. He added two wire baskets, one above the other. The baskets were not permanently attached to the carrier. In the store, the carriers were folded against a wall with the baskets stacked nearby. Goldman called the new invention a "shopping cart."

Goldman started the Folding Carrier Basket Company to make more carts. The shopping cart did not catch on at first. In some stores, owners paid models to shop with the carts to give customers the idea.

One of the first improvements to the cart was to attach the baskets permanently to the carrier. Shoppers began putting their children in them. In 1947 a child seat became part of the cart. Later, a piece of plastic was added to close the leg holes so that shoppers could put small items there without having them fall out. Companies began making carts in colors with the store names on them. They added rubber wheels that swiveled. Today's shopping carts are larger and look much different from the early ones.

1. **Recognizing Words in Context**

   Find the word *convenient* in the passage. One definition below is closest to the meaning of that word. One definition has the opposite or nearly the opposite meaning. The remaining definition has a completely different meaning. Label the definitions C for *closest*, O for *opposite or nearly opposite*, and D for *different*.

   _____ a. difficult

   _____ b. handy

   _____ c. stressful

2. **Distinguishing Fact from Opinion**

   Two of the statements below present *facts*, which can be proved. The other statement is an *opinion*, which expresses someone's thoughts or beliefs. Label the statements F for *fact* and O for *opinion*.

   _____ a. Larger carts are better than smaller carts.

   _____ b. The first shopping-cart frame was made from a folding chair.

   _____ c. Sylvan Goldman started the Folding Carrier Basket Company.

3. Keeping Events in Order

Number the statements below 1, 2, and 3 to show the order in which the events took place.

_____ a. A child seat was added to shopping carts.

_____ b. Sylvan Goldman built the first shopping cart.

_____ c. Sylvan Goldman started a company to make shopping carts.

4. Making Correct Inferences

Two of the statements below are correct *inferences,* or reasonable guesses. They are based on information in the passage. The other statement is an incorrect, or faulty, inference. Label the statements C for *correct* inference and F for *faulty* inference.

_____ a. Sylvan Goldman was a creative problem solver.

_____ b. Without shopping carts, there would be no grocery stores.

_____ c. Today's shopping cart is much improved from the first carrier.

5. Understanding Main Ideas

One of the statements below expresses the main idea of the passage. One statement is too general, or too broad. The other explains only part of the passage; it is too narrow. Label the statements M for *main idea*, B for *too broad*, and N for *too narrow.*

_____ a. Sylvan Goldman was one of many inventors during the 1930s.

_____ b. Sylvan Goldman invented the shopping cart in 1937 and continued to improve it over the years.

_____ c. The shopping cart did not catch on at first.

Correct Answers, Part A _____

Correct Answers, Part B _____

Total Correct Answers _____

Life in the New England Colonies

Before there was a United States, there were the English colonies. These were located along the East Coast. They would later become the first 13 states.

Life in the colonies was different in many ways from present-day life in the states. Today, more people live and work in cities and towns than on farms. In colonial times, although some people lived in towns, many lived on farms. They used oxen to plow their fields. They raised food crops such as wheat, corn, barley, and oats. They raised cash crops, such as tobacco, that they would sell to get money. They also raised livestock, such as cows, pigs, sheep, and chickens. They made most of the things they needed them-selves. They bought or traded the things that they could not make. Like many farmers today, colonial farmers often worked at other jobs. A farmer might also be a house builder, a well digger, or a craftsman.

Colonial families were different as well. Today's families tend to be small. Colonial families usually had many children. A family with 16 children was common. The family treated children over the age of six like small adults. The children wore adult clothes and helped with the work. Children fed the livestock, worked in the fields, and cut and carried in firewood. They worked before and after school. Some boys worked in shops, learning a trade; other boys went to sea in the ships that came and went from England. Girls learned "women's work" from their mothers. They sewed and mended clothes, spun wool into yarn, made brooms from straw, and wove baskets. They milked the cows and made cheese and butter.

Colonial children also grew up faster than children do today. Boys were considered grown up at age 16. They paid taxes and served in the militia, which was the local army. People expected girls to be married by age 18. They were often married as early as age 16.

Today people often go to parties to have fun. The colonists had fun too, but their social gatherings revolved around church and work. People visited after church. Men got together to help build a barn or harvest the crops. Women got together to spin yarn or make a quilt. Sometimes the colonists celebrated a day of Thanksgiving, such as people celebrate today. Colonial people, like people today, believed that they had much to be thankful for.

Reading Time _____

Recalling Facts

1. The English colonies were located
   - ❑ a. along the East Coast.
   - ❑ b. in England.
   - ❑ c. in the West.

2. The English colonies would later become
   - ❑ a. large cities.
   - ❑ b. the states of Virginia, Ohio, and Massachusetts.
   - ❑ c. the first 13 states.

3. Colonial women made brooms from
   - ❑ a. straw.
   - ❑ b. yarn.
   - ❑ c. wheat.

4. Most social activities in the colonies were related to
   - ❑ a. church and work.
   - ❑ b. school.
   - ❑ c. the militia.

5. In colonial times, boys were thought to be grown up at age
   - ❑ a. 12.
   - ❑ b. 16.
   - ❑ c. 18.

Understanding Ideas

6. After reading the information in the passage, one can conclude that the colonists
   - ❑ a. worked very hard and helped one another.
   - ❑ b. did not socialize with their neighbors.
   - ❑ c. pampered their children.

7. A colonial girl would not be likely to
   - ❑ a. learn a trade.
   - ❑ b. milk the cows.
   - ❑ c. mend clothes.

8. From information in the passage, one can conclude that colonial children over the age of six
   - ❑ a. led carefree lives.
   - ❑ b. worked hard all day.
   - ❑ c. went to war.

9. In contrast to children in the United States today, colonial children were more likely to
   - ❑ a. have a dozen brothers and sisters.
   - ❑ b. give parties for their friends.
   - ❑ c. have their own bedrooms.

10. Social gatherings in the colonies probably centered around work because
    - ❑ a. most people owed large debts to their neighbors.
    - ❑ b. the early colonists did not believe that people should have fun and enjoy life.
    - ❑ c. there was always much work to do.

3 B Mary Chilton: The First Person to Land at Plymouth Rock

A famous painting called "The Landing of the Pilgrims" shows people in a small boat by a rocky shore. A young girl is stepping from the boat onto a large rock. The year was 1620, and the girl was Mary Chilton. According to legend, she was the first person to set foot on Plymouth Rock in the New World.

Historians do not know when or where Chilton was born. Her family lived in Holland for a time. They went to England with a group of Pilgrims to set sail on the Mayflower. People in England did not accept the Pilgrims' religion. The Pilgrims wanted to go to the New World to live with religious freedom.

The Mayflower set sail for Jamestown, Virginia. It never got there but, instead, was anchored for a time in Cape Cod Bay. During this time, Mary Chilton's father died. The Mayflower finally found a harbor across the bay. Some people went ashore there in a small boat called a launch. One story says that Mary Chilton raced John Alden to the front of the launch to be first out of the boat.

It was winter when the Pilgrims landed at Plymouth. Soon after that, Mary Chilton's mother died. Mary then lived with another family.

Mary Chilton grew up and married John Winslow. The Winslows moved to Boston and had 10 children.

1. **Recognizing Words in Context**

   Find the word *anchored* in the passage. One definition below is closest to the meaning of that word. One definition has the opposite or nearly the opposite meaning. The remaining definition has a completely different meaning. Label the definitions C for *closest*, O for *opposite or nearly opposite*, and D for *different*.

   _____ a. moved

   _____ b. held in place

   _____ c. swayed

2. **Distinguishing Fact from Opinion**

   Two of the statements below present *facts*, which can be proved. The other statement is an *opinion*, which expresses someone's thoughts or beliefs. Label the statements F for *fact* and O for *opinion*.

   _____ a. The Mayflower landed at Plymouth Rock in 1620.

   _____ b. Mary Chilton married John Winslow.

   _____ c. Mary should have let an adult get off the boat first.

23

3. Keeping Events in Order

Number the statements below 1, 2, and 3 to show the order in which the events took place.

_____ a. The Mayflower anchored in Cape Cod Bay.

_____ b. The Mayflower finally found a harbor across the bay.

_____ c. The Mayflower set sail for Jamestown.

4. Making Correct Inferences

Two of the statements below are correct *inferences,* or reasonable guesses. They are based on information in the passage. The other statement is an incorrect, or faulty, inference. Label the statements C for *correct* inference and F for *faulty* inference.

_____ a. Mary Chilton wanted to be first off the boat so that she could be famous.

_____ b. Mary Chilton traveled a long way and suffered hardships.

_____ c. People in England tried to keep the Pilgrims from practicing their religion.

5. Understanding Main Ideas

One of the statements below expresses the main idea of the passage. One statement is too general, or too broad. The other explains only part of the passage; it is too narrow. Label the statements M for *main idea,* B for *too broad,* and N for *too narrow.*

_____ a. Many Pilgrims from England journeyed to the New World.

_____ b. Mary Chilton sailed to the New World on the Mayflower and was the first person to set foot on Plymouth Rock.

_____ c. Mary Chilton married John Winslow.

Correct Answers, Part A _____

Correct Answers, Part B _____

Total Correct Answers _____

Before 1840 people made buildings from stone, brick, or wood. The outside walls carried the weight of the building. A building more than a few stories tall became very heavy. A tall building, such as a castle, had very thick walls.

By 1850 builders were using iron for the fronts of some large buildings. Iron is lighter than stone and stronger than wood. Raw iron found in the earth is not strong enough for use in buildings. The type of iron used in building structures is called an alloy.

An alloy is a metal made by melting and mixing different metals and other compounds. Iron is made in a blast furnace, a tall chamber lined with brick and open at the top. Workers feed limestone, iron ore, and coke (made from coal) into the top. Near the bottom, hot air is forced in. The hot air and a chemical reaction turn the materials into a molten (liquid) mass. The waste, called slag, is drawn off, leaving the iron. The hot iron is formed into large blocks called pigs. The pigs can be formed to make objects. This formed iron is called cast iron.

Cast iron is strong, but it still contains unwanted elements. People knew that removing these impurities would result in a stronger material. To do this, they needed to heat the iron to very high temperatures, but the blast furnace could not make that much heat.

In England, Sir Henry Bessemer found the solution. He forced air through molten pig iron. The oxygen in the air mixed with the impurities in the iron in a process called oxidation. When oxidation takes place, it makes heat. The heat turns impurities into slag. Pure steel, which is much stronger than iron, is produced. The Bessemer process took place in an egg-shaped converter. Through this process, a large amount of steel could be made quickly and cheaply.

By the late 1800s, many people were living and working in big cities. The price of land rose. As land grew more expensive, builders looked for ways to lower costs. Taller buildings saved on land cost. In Chicago, George A. Fuller built the Tacoma building. It was a structure in which the outside walls did not carry all of the weight. Fuller used steel beams to make cages that carried the weight of the building. Soon more tall buildings of 10 to 20 stories appeared. These were the first skyscrapers.

Reading Time _____

Recalling Facts

1. Before 1840 most buildings were built of
   - ❑ a. iron.
   - ❑ b. stone, brick, or wood.
   - ❑ c. steel.

2. Iron used in buildings is
   - ❑ a. not as strong as wood.
   - ❑ b. raw iron.
   - ❑ c. an alloy.

3. Iron is made in
   - ❑ a. a blast furnace.
   - ❑ b. an egg-shaped furnace.
   - ❑ c. the open air.

4. In the Bessemer process,
   - ❑ a. lower temperatures are used for making cast iron.
   - ❑ b. iron is melted in a blast furnace.
   - ❑ c. air is forced through pig iron.

5. The first skyscrapers were
   - ❑ a. 5 to 6 stories high.
   - ❑ b. 10 to 20 stories high.
   - ❑ c. 30 to 50 stories high.

Understanding Ideas

6. From the article, one can conclude that the Bessemer process led to
   - ❑ a. more populated cities, with people living and working on less land.
   - ❑ b. fewer pollution problems in cities.
   - ❑ c. a greater number of people moving back to farmland.

7. Bessemer's process was most likely a success because it
   - ❑ a. made iron from steel.
   - ❑ b. made lots of steel quickly and cheaply.
   - ❑ c. produced less slag than a blast furnace.

8. From the article, one can conclude that alloys are important because they
   - ❑ a. have properties that are more desirable than the separate metals they are made from.
   - ❑ b. have no impurities.
   - ❑ c. are the raw elements from which iron is made.

9. From reading the passage, one can conclude that Bessemer
   - ❑ a. knew how to make cast iron.
   - ❑ b. avoided difficult problems.
   - ❑ c. was not familiar with metals like steel.

10. From reading the passage, one can conclude that architects throughout history
    - ❑ a. could not design creative buildings until steel was invented.
    - ❑ b. disliked using stone, bricks, and wood.
    - ❑ c. thought carefully about available materials when designing buildings.

4 B The Flatiron Building

The Flatiron Building was the first skyscraper built in New York City. It is 21 stories high and sits at the intersection of 23rd Street and Broadway and Fifth Avenues. The three streets meet at a sharp angle, and the lot formed by the streets is a narrow triangle.

In about 1900, Daniel H. Burnham designed a tall building to fit the shape of the lot. The corner of the building where the streets meet is just six feet wide. The building was one of the first to have a steel frame. The Fuller Construction Company built it and then moved its offices there, naming the building the Fuller Building. During its construction, people called it "Burnham's Folly." They thought its height and narrow shape would cause it to fall.

The building did not fall, and it still stands today. When it was completed, people nicknamed it the Flatiron Building. Its triangular shape made them think of a flatiron, a tool used to press clothes.

The steel frame of the building is covered with a limestone face. The building looks a bit like a tall wedge with three sections. Columns and carved flowers adorn the lowest and highest floors. The middle floors have a wavelike design. Today, many taller skyscrapers surround the Flatiron Building. Still, it is one of the most famous buildings in the city.

1. **Recognizing Words in Context**

   Find the word *adorn* in the passage. One definition below is closest to the meaning of that word. One definition has the opposite or nearly the opposite meaning. The remaining definition has a completely different meaning. Label the definitions C for *closest*, O for *opposite or nearly opposite*, and D for *different*.

   _____ a. simplify

   _____ b. clutter

   _____ c. decorate

2. **Distinguishing Fact from Opinion**

   Two of the statements below present *facts*, which can be proved. The other statement is an *opinion*, which expresses someone's thoughts or beliefs. Label the statements F for *fact* and O for *opinion*.

   _____ a. The Flatiron Building was New York City's first skyscraper.

   _____ b. The Flatiron Building is 21 stories high.

   _____ c. Today's skyscrapers are too tall.

3. Keeping Events in Order

Number the statements below 1, 2, and 3 to show the order in which the events took place.

_____ a. The Fuller Construction Company moved its offices to the Flatiron Building.

_____ b. People called the building "Burnham's Folly."

_____ c. Burnham designed a tall building to fit a lot in the shape of a triangle.

4. Making Correct Inferences

Two of the statements below are correct *inferences,* or reasonable guesses. They are based on information in the passage. The other statement is an incorrect, or faulty, inference. Label the statements C for *correct* inference and F for *faulty* inference.

_____ a. People today still refer to the Flatiron Building as "Burnham's Folly."

_____ b. The Flatiron Building is strong because of its steel frame.

_____ c. The Flatiron Building is unusual because of its shape.

5. Understanding Main Ideas

One of the statements below expresses the main idea of the passage. One statement is too general, or too broad. The other explains only part of the passage; it is too narrow. Label the statements M for *main idea,* B for *too broad,* and N for *too narrow.*

_____ a. Made of steel and lime-stone, the unusual Flatiron Building was New York City's first skyscraper.

_____ b. Skyscrapers have brought many changes to the land-scape of New York City.

_____ c. The Flatiron Building has a steel frame with a lime-stone face.

Correct Answers, Part A _____

Correct Answers, Part B _____

Total Correct Answers _____

Robert Peary and Matthew Henson: Arctic Explorers

In 1886 explorer Robert Peary traveled to Greenland for the U.S. Navy. Before his journey, no one knew Greenland's size or shape. On Peary's first trips, he explored Greenland, mapping parts of it.

When Peary returned to the United States, he went to a furrier to sell some furs. There he met Matthew Henson, an African American mechanic, builder, and navigator. When Peary went to Nicaragua on a Navy mission, Henson went with him. When that job was over, the two headed to the Arctic.

Henson and Peary set sail for Greenland. When they landed, Henson built a house for their base camp. Peary and his men set out to explore the terrain by dog sledge (a heavy sled). Henson was injured and had to stay at the base. While there, he became friends with the Inuit, the native people. He became an expert in building sledges and handling dogs.

In 1895 Henson, Peary, and Hugh Lee went out on another dog sledge expedition. This time, they found Greenland's northernmost point. They now knew that the North Pole lay under the frozen Arctic Sea. Peary had hoped to cross the ice, but the group ran out of food and returned to base camp. In the years that followed, Peary and Henson tried several times to reach the North Pole, but each time they failed. On one trip, Peary's feet froze, and he lost his toes.

Peary and Henson planned one last trip when Peary was 53 years old. They started across the sea ice from Ellesmere Island, which is located north of Canada. The explorers formed small, alternating teams that set out days apart. The first team broke the trail, built igloos, left food, and then went back for more supplies. The next team used the food and forged ahead. The temperature dropped as low as –60 degrees Fahrenheit (–51 degrees Celsius). The explorers' cheeks froze, and they suffered snow blindness from the sun's glare. They weathered high winds and storms, and they also faced a hidden danger. Under the frozen ocean are powerful currents. The ice moves and breaks apart leaving open water, called leads. Twice Peary fell into leads. About 140 miles from the North Pole, the last support team turned back. Henson and Peary went on with four Inuit and 40 dogs. Five days later, they became the first persons to reach the North Pole.

Reading Time _____

Recalling Facts

1. Peary met Henson
   - ❑ a. at a furrier's in the United States.
   - ❑ b. in a camp in Greenland.
   - ❑ c. on a ship in Nicaragua.

2. Henson
   - ❑ a. was born in Greenland.
   - ❑ b. traveled to Greenland in 1886 for the U.S. Navy.
   - ❑ c. traveled to Greenland with Peary.

3. Snow blindness is caused by
   - ❑ a. ice forming on the eyelids.
   - ❑ b. the sun's glare on the snow.
   - ❑ c. high winds.

4. A lead is
   - ❑ a. open water formed by ice's moving and breaking apart.
   - ❑ b. part of a sledge dog harness.
   - ❑ c. a supply igloo.

5. In 1895 Henson, Peary, and Hugh Lee found
   - ❑ a. Ellesmere Island.
   - ❑ b. an unknown area north of Canada.
   - ❑ c. Greenland's northernmost point.

Understanding Ideas

6. From reading the passage, one can infer that Arctic travel is
   - ❑ a. cold and dangerous.
   - ❑ b. fast because sledges slide over the ice easily.
   - ❑ c. not possible over sea ice.

7. Peary most likely chose Henson to go with him to the North Pole because Henson was
   - ❑ a. a furrier who was once a Naval officer.
   - ❑ b. the only one who volunteered.
   - ❑ c. a mechanic, builder, and navigator.

8. One can infer that Peary and Henson were
   - ❑ a. reckless and careless.
   - ❑ b. determined, adventurous, and brave.
   - ❑ c. working hard so that they could become famous.

9. From the passage, one can infer that Peary and Henson
   - ❑ a. were relieved to find out that the journey was much easier than they had expected.
   - ❑ b. worked well as a team.
   - ❑ c. reached the North Pole more than once.

10. The last trip by Peary and Henson was probably successful because
    - ❑ a. the weather then was warmer than on their earlier trips.
    - ❑ b. they used the information that they had gained from their earlier trips.
    - ❑ c. they faced no hidden dangers.

Dog sledges are an important means of Arctic travel. A sledge consists of two long runners with crossbars. The front curves upward, and lines from the front of the sledge attach to the dogs' harnesses. The driver stands on the runners and shouts orders to the dogs.

The Inuit people of the Arctic first made sledges from wood, ivory, horn, or whale's teeth. They made the lines and harnesses from sealskin or other hides.

Explorers such as Robert Peary and Matthew Henson used sledges on their Arctic trips. They made them from wood and steel runners. Teams of 6 to 12 Inuit sledge dogs pulled the sledges. These dogs first came to the Arctic from Asia with the ancestors of the Inuit.

Inuit dogs have large, round paws with strong nails and thick pads, which enable them to run over ice and snow. The dogs have a double coat. The outer coat has long hairs and the undercoat is thick and wooly. The dogs can sleep in the open under extremely cold conditions. They can keep going through storms. Strong hips, large thigh muscles, and powerful chests help the dogs pull heavy loads. Peary and Henson's sledges carried about 650 pounds (295 kilograms).

People in remote parts of Alaska and Greenland still use dog sledges to carry goods and mail.

1. **Recognizing Words in Context**

    Find the word *remote* in the passage. One definition below is closest to the meaning of that word. One definition has the opposite or nearly the opposite meaning. The remaining definition has a completely different meaning. Label the definitions C for *closest*, O for *opposite or nearly opposite*, and D for *different*.

    _____ a. faraway

    _____ b. nearby

    _____ c. gentle

2. **Distinguishing Fact from Opinion**

    Two of the statements below present *facts*, which can be proved. The other statement is an *opinion*, which expresses someone's thoughts or beliefs. Label the statements F for *fact* and O for *opinion*.

    _____ a. Sledges made from wood are better than those made from whale's teeth.

    _____ b. Inuit sledge dogs have a double coat of fur.

    _____ c. Early sledges had lines and harnesses made from sealskin.

3. **Keeping Events in Order**

   Number the statements below 1, 2, and 3 to show the order in which the events took place.

   _____ a. Sledge dogs come to the Arctic from Asia.

   _____ b. Explorers Peary and Henson used sledge dogs on their Arctic trips.

   _____ c. People in remote parts of Alaska still use dog sledges to carry mail.

4. **Making Correct Inferences**

   Two of the statements below are correct *inferences,* or reasonable guesses. They are based on information in the passage. The other statement is an incorrect, or faulty, inference. Label the statements C for *correct* inference and F for *faulty* inference.

   _____ a. Inuit sledge dogs are well adapted to the Arctic environment.

   _____ b. Peary and Henson's Arctic explorations would have been almost impossible without dog sledges.

   _____ c. Sledge dogs are strong but do not work well in teams.

5. **Understanding Main Ideas**

   One of the statements below expresses the main idea of the passage. One statement is too general, or too broad. The other explains only part of the passage; it is too narrow. Label the statements M for *main idea,* B for *too broad,* and N for *too narrow.*

   _____ a. Dog sledges are used in the Arctic.

   _____ b. Dog sledges are an important form of Arctic transportation, ideally suited to the harsh environment.

   _____ c. Teams of 6 to 12 Inuit sledge dogs pulled Peary's sledges.

Correct Answers, Part A _____

Correct Answers, Part B _____

Total Correct Answers _____

Newspapers are one method of bringing the news to the public. Reporters, photographers, correspondents, and editors are some of the people who create newspapers. They are known as journalists.

Reporters are journalists who go out and get the news. They attend meetings. They cover events such as court cases, plays, and sports events. They interview people to get their views of what is going on. They jot down notes and quotations to use in writing the story. Reporters must be able to write a story quickly so as to meet a deadline. People do not want to read old news. They want to know what is going on as soon as it happens. Reporters sometimes phone or e-mail their notes and quotations to the paper from the scene. A reporter at the paper then writes the story.

A "stringer" is a part-time reporter who works when called upon. A fire might break out in one part of town. An editor may ask a stringer who lives near the scene to cover the story.

Reporters often work with photographers, or photojournalists. Photo-journalists take the pictures that illustrate the stories in a newspaper. They have to develop their film in time for the pictures to appear with the story.

A correspondent is a journalist who covers the news in a particular place or on a subject that he or she has expertise in. Large newspaper groups have correspondents who cover government news in Washington, D.C. They have correspondents in foreign countries to report the news there. A paper may have a correspondent who covers just medical news.

An editor is a journalist who works at a desk in a newspaper office. Editors prepare the reporters' stories to be printed in the paper. They decide which story is most important and gets the front page headline. They decide which pictures to use. Large papers have an editor for each section. Editors do not often write the news, but they do write editorials in which they state their views on a topic or an issue.

People who work as journalists have some things in common. They are curious, they like to write, and they have a "nose for news." They can spot news as it happens. They know what people want to read about.

A person who wants to be a journalist usually needs a college degree and some job experience. One way to get experience is to work on a college paper.

Reading Time _____

Recalling Facts

1. Reporters
   - ❑ a. go out and get the news.
   - ❑ b. develop film.
   - ❑ c. edit news stories.

2. A stringer is
   - ❑ a. a part-time reporter who works when called upon.
   - ❑ b. an editor.
   - ❑ c. a photojournalist.

3. An editorial is
   - ❑ a. the story that gets the front page headline.
   - ❑ b. a news story written by an editor.
   - ❑ c. a piece that expresses an editor's view on a topic.

4. A correspondent
   - ❑ a. teaches journalism.
   - ❑ b. reports the news in a particular place or on a subject that he or she has expertise in.
   - ❑ c. decides which story is most important.

5. When a big story breaks in a foreign country, the journalist most likely to get the news first is
   - ❑ a. a stringer.
   - ❑ b. a correspondent.
   - ❑ c. an editor.

Understanding Ideas

6. From reading the passage, one can conclude that
   - ❑ a. reporters have the most important job in getting the news to the public.
   - ❑ b. getting the news to the public is a team effort.
   - ❑ c. reporters are better writers than editors.

7. From the information given, one can conclude that journalists
   - ❑ a. must have good writing skills.
   - ❑ b. can usually send in stories by telephone or audiotape.
   - ❑ c. are the least important members of a newspaper team.

8. Of the following, it is probably most important that a photojournalist
   - ❑ a. call the editor to discuss what pictures to take.
   - ❑ b. take good pictures and develop them quickly.
   - ❑ c. have more than one camera.

9. From information in the passage, one can conclude that
   - ❑ a. time is not an important factor when writing news events.
   - ❑ b. most newspaper reporters do not need to work well under pressure.
   - ❑ c. stories must be written well and on time, usually on the day of the news event.

10. From the passage, one can conclude that large newspaper groups have an advantage over small newspapers in
    - ❑ a. editing stories accurately.
    - ❑ b. covering breaking news from around the world.
    - ❑ c. reporting on local sports teams.

People read newspaper articles to find out what is going on. A person can write a top quality newspaper article by following six steps.

Step One: Choose a topic people want to read about or need to know about. Some examples are current events, community issues, and sports news.

Step Two: Get the facts. Ask the questions who, what, where, when, and how. Find eyewitnesses or experts and interview them. Write down their words exactly so that they can be quoted in the story. Cover both sides of an issue. For example, should an old house be demolished to make room for a playground? Or should it be repaired and used as a museum?

Step Three: Organize the material. Decide what is important. A story about a baseball game would tell which teams played, where they played, who won, and what the final score was. Interviews with coaches, highlights of the game, and quotations from fans would add more interest.

Step Four: Write a draft. Start with a topic sentence that sums up the main idea and then write the details, including quotations from interviews.

Step Five: Revise and edit. Read the story aloud to be sure it makes sense. Check for spelling and grammar errors.

Step Six: Write a headline that gets people's attention and tells what the story is about.

1. **Recognizing Words in Context**

   Find the word *demolished* in the passage. One definition below is closest to the meaning of that word. One definition has the opposite or nearly the opposite meaning. The remaining definition has a completely different meaning. Label the definitions C for *closest*, O for *opposite or nearly opposite*, and D for *different*.

   _____ a. built

   _____ b. torn down

   _____ c. reminded

2. **Distinguishing Fact from Opinion**

   Two of the statements below present *facts*, which can be proved. The other statement is an *opinion*, which expresses someone's thoughts or beliefs. Label the statements F for *fact* and O for *opinion*.

   _____ a. Articles on sports are more interesting than articles on community issues.

   _____ b. News articles are written about community issues, current events, and sports.

   _____ c. A headline is a short announcement that gets attention.

3. Keeping Events in Order

Number the statements below 1, 2, and 3 to show the order in which the events took place.

_____ a. Write a draft.

_____ b. Get the facts.

_____ c. Organize the material.

4. Making Correct Inferences

Two of the statements below are correct *inferences,* or reasonable guesses. They are based on information in the passage. The other statement is an incorrect, or faulty, inference. Label the statements C for *correct* inference and F for *faulty* inference.

_____ a. Most news articles are about community issues.

_____ b. The purpose of news articles is to inform readers.

_____ c. A good article includes the most important facts about a topic.

5. Understanding Main Ideas

One of the statements below expresses the main idea of the passage. One statement is too general, or too broad. The other explains only part of the passage; it is too narrow. Label the statements M for *main idea,* B for *too broad,* and N for *too narrow.*

_____ a. Follow these six steps to write a good newspaper article.

_____ b. Interview experts to get quotations when writing a news article.

_____ c. Newspapers are a good source of information.

Correct Answers, Part A _____

Correct Answers, Part B _____

Total Correct Answers _____

The Swiss Alps

The Alps are a large mountain chain in Western Europe. The entire chain spans some 750 miles (1200 km). The Swiss Alps are the western part of the Alps.

The Alps were formed by movement of the earth's surface, or crust. The crust is made up of sections, called plates. Millions of years ago, the plate under Africa moved against the plate under Europe and Asia, forcing rock to pile up in huge folds. As the pressure continued, the rock folded over itself. This made overlapping folds, or pleats. This is called a fold-mountain system. The process took place over millions of years.

The Alps have been further shaped by wind, water, and ice. Wind and water have worn away some of the rock. Water flowing down the mountains has cut through the rock, making riverbeds. Water gets into cracks in the rock and freezes, causing the rock to split. This has made very unusually shaped peaks. Glaciers have carved the valleys into deep channels. Ice masses have formed dams across rivers, causing lakes to form. The glaciers have worn away the sides of some mountain peaks, leaving them with steep sides. Such a peak is called a horn. One example of a famous horn is the Matterhorn in the Swiss Alps.

Switzerland is often called the "land of the Alps" because mountains cover about 60 percent of the land. The Swiss Alps are higher and narrower than the eastern Alps. The Rhone and Rhine are two of Europe's major rivers. Their valleys divide the Swiss Alps into north and south. Most of the Swiss population lives in the river valleys or on the large plain between the Alps and the Jura Mountains. The Jura Mountains are a branch of the Alps.

The temperature in the Swiss Alps varies with the elevation: the higher up the mountain, the lower the temperature. The tallest peaks are snow covered year round, but in the valleys it can be quite warm in the summer.

Because the Alps are mostly wilderness, they support much wildlife. Wolves, foxes, lynx, deer, and mountain goats live in the forests, valleys, and grassy pastures. The clear mountain lakes are home to fish, swans, ducks, and seagulls. Rare plants and flowers grow in the high meadows.

People from all over the world come to see the Swiss Alps. They come to hike, ski, climb challenging peaks, fish in crystal clear lakes, and photograph nature.

Reading Time _____

Recalling Facts

1. The Alps were formed by
   - ❑ a. volcanoes.
   - ❑ b. the movement of the earth's surface.
   - ❑ c. the Rhone and Rhine Rivers.

2. When the Alps were formed, rock folded over itself, making overlapping
   - ❑ a. pleats.
   - ❑ b. horns.
   - ❑ c. peaks.

3. Mountains cover about _____ percent of the land in Switzerland.
   - ❑ a. 20
   - ❑ b. 40
   - ❑ c. 60

4. Most of the Swiss population lives
   - ❑ a. in the river valleys or on the large plain.
   - ❑ b. high in the mountains.
   - ❑ c. on the Alpine meadows.

5. The Jura Mountains are
   - ❑ a. the largest mountain range in Europe.
   - ❑ b. a branch of the Alps.
   - ❑ c. a series of glaciers.

Understanding Ideas

6. Which of these sentences tells what the whole passage is about?
   - ❑ a. The Swiss Alps are a mountain chain that provides rugged wilderness, valleys to live in, and many vacation opportunities.
   - ❑ b. The Alps are a famous mountain chain in Western Europe.
   - ❑ c. Mountains cover about 60 percent of Switzerland.

7. From the passage, one can infer that the Alps
   - ❑ a. are located entirely in Switzerland.
   - ❑ b. extend through more than one country.
   - ❑ c. are on more than one continent.

8. From the passage, one can infer that the shape of the Alps
   - ❑ a. changes noticeably from one year to the next.
   - ❑ b. never changes.
   - ❑ c. continues to change slowly over time.

9. From the passage, one can infer that most of the people live in the river valleys or on the plain because
   - ❑ a. the land there is flatter.
   - ❑ b. there are wolves and lynx in the mountains.
   - ❑ c. fishing is better in the rivers than in the mountain lakes.

10. If a person were walking in the Swiss Alps and the temperature were gradually warming, the person would most likely be
    - ❑ a. walking through a snowfield.
    - ❑ b. climbing up the mountain.
    - ❑ c. going down the mountain.

Climbing the Swiss Alps: The "4,000ers"

The earliest people to climb mountains did so to explore. In the 1700s, people began to climb mountains, such as the Alps, for sport. By 1900 mountain climbing clubs had formed. The Swiss Alps include more than 80 peaks that are at least 4,000 meters (about 13,000 feet) high. These peaks are called the "4,000ers," and they make the Swiss Alps a mountain climber's paradise.

The highest mountain in the Swiss Alps is Monte Rosa. Its summit, or highest peak, is the Dufourspitze. It takes about three days for an expert climber to reach the top. From the top, the view is boundless: one can see snow-covered peaks all the way to France and Italy.

The Matterhorn is the best-known Swiss peak. Edward Whymper from England was the first climber to ascend to its top. Whymper tried and failed many times, but in 1865 he and a group of climbers and guides finally made the summit. On the way down, one climber fell and a rope broke, causing four men to fall to their deaths. In 1871 Lucy Walker was the first woman to make thc climb.

Today climbers come from all over the world to climb in the Swiss Alps. New equipment and a network of fixed ropes in difficult places make climbing safer. Nevertheless, storms, fog, and rockslides can threaten climbers.

1. **Recognizing Words in Context**

   Find the word *ascend* in the passage. One definition below is closest to the meaning of that word. One definition has the opposite or nearly the opposite meaning. The remaining definition has a completely different meaning. Label the definitions C for *closest,* O for *opposite or nearly opposite,* and D for *different.*

   _____ a. cross

   _____ b. come down

   _____ c. move upward

2. **Distinguishing Fact from Opinion**

   Two of the statements below present *facts,* which can be proved. The other statement is an *opinion,* which expresses someone's thoughts or beliefs. Label the statements F for *fact* and O for *opinion.*

   _____ a. The highest mountain in the Swiss Alps is Monte Rosa.

   _____ b. People shouldn't climb mountains because of the dangers.

   _____ c. Edward Whymper was the first to climb to the top of the Matterhorn.

3. Keeping Events in Order

Number the statements below 1, 2, and 3 to show the order in which the events took place.

_____ a. In the 1700s, people first climbed mountains for sport.

_____ b. By 1900 mountain climbing clubs had formed.

_____ c. The first people to climb mountains did so to explore.

4. Making Correct Inferences

Two of the statements below are correct *inferences,* or reasonable guesses. They are based on information in the passage. The other statement is an incorrect, or faulty, inference. Label the statements C for *correct* inference and F for *faulty* inference.

_____ a. Mountain climbing is safer today than in the 1700s.

_____ b. One reason people climb to the top of a mountain is to see the view.

_____ c. With new kinds of equipment, today climbing the Swiss Alps is easy.

5. Understanding Main Ideas

One of the statements below expresses the main idea of the passage. One statement is too general, or too broad. The other explains only part of the passage; it is too narrow. Label the statements M for *main idea*, B for *too broad*, and N for *too narrow*.

_____ a. The Matterhorn is the best-known Swiss peak.

_____ b. Switzerland's famous 4,000-meter-high peaks attract many mountain climbers.

_____ c. People must train to climb mountains.

Correct Answers, Part A _____

Correct Answers, Part B _____

Total Correct Answers _____

How to Read a Map

How do people get to where they want to go? How far away is it from here to there? One can find the answers to these questions and many others by using a map. A map is a drawing of an area, such as a state or country. Maps show mountains, cities, rivers, and oceans. They may show roads and other features. They also show directions and distance.

Maps show directions with a compass rose, which is a circle with a star inside it. The points of the "star" show the directions of north, east, south, and west, and those in-between, such as northeast. The compass is called a rose because the compass points drawn through the circle resemble the petals of a rose.

Maps show distance with a scale, which is a line that resembles a ruler. The lines on the scale mark off miles, kilometers, or other units of measure. On some maps, the scale shows how many miles an inch or a centimeter stands for on the map. Maps also have colors and symbols. The map key is a small chart that tells what the colors and symbols stand for.

World maps and globes include a grid of lines. Although a world map is flat, a globe is a sphere, like Earth. On a globe, one can easily see how this imaginary grid divides Earth. The horizontal lines are latitudes. They are also called parallels because they are an equal distance apart. A map or globe shows latitude in degrees from 0 to 90. The line around the equator is zero degrees. The equator divides Earth into a northern half and a southern half. The degrees increase to the north and south. The North Pole is 90 degrees north, and the South Pole is 90 degrees south.

Longitude lines are the vertical lines. They are also called meridians. They run from pole to pole. They are farthest apart from one another at the equator. They get closer to each other as they near the poles. The line that runs through Greenwich, England, is zero degrees. The degrees continue to 180 east and west, where they meet in the Pacific Ocean.

Any point on a world map or globe can be described in terms of latitude and longitude. A point that is 30 degrees north of the equator and 70 degrees west of the zero meridian is written *30°N, 70°W.*

Reading Time _____

Recalling Facts

1. Maps show direction with a
   - ❑ a. compass rose.
   - ❑ b. meridian.
   - ❑ c. degree.

2. Maps show distance with
   - ❑ a. symbols.
   - ❑ b. a scale.
   - ❑ c. a compass rose.

3. A map key
   - ❑ a. explains what symbols and colors on the map mean.
   - ❑ b. is in the shape of a key.
   - ❑ c. shows latitude and longitude.

4. Latitude lines are also called parallels because
   - ❑ a. they are measured in degrees from 0 to 90.
   - ❑ b. they are farthest apart at the equator.
   - ❑ c. they are an equal distance apart.

5. Longitude lines are
   - ❑ a. parallel.
   - ❑ b. horizontal.
   - ❑ c. vertical.

Understanding Ideas

6. If one is planning a vacation by car, a map is least likely to help
   - ❑ a. choose the shortest route.
   - ❑ b. find the closest gas station.
   - ❑ c. find a place near water to visit.

7. To find out how far it is from Cleveland, Ohio, to Columbus, Ohio, one would
   - ❑ a. measure the distance on the map and then compare it to the map scale.
   - ❑ b. find the latitude of each city.
   - ❑ c. use the compass rose to find out which direction Columbus is from Cleveland.

8. If one wanted to find a park on a city map, he or she would
   - ❑ a. use the grid to find the center of the city.
   - ❑ b. use the map key to find the symbol for a park.
   - ❑ c. start at the top left corner and search it from left to right.

9. The designation 40°S, 50°E indicates a point on a world map that is
   - ❑ a. south of Greenwich, England, and east of the equator.
   - ❑ b. south of the equator and east of Greenwich, England.
   - ❑ c. south of the North Pole and east of the South Pole.

10. From reading the passage, one can infer that
   - ❑ a. maps are mostly useful in social studies class.
   - ❑ b. maps are not so useful as remembering landmarks is.
   - ❑ c. maps help us to understand locations and distance.

Climate is a term for the average weather through the course of the year at a certain place. A variety of factors affect the climate of an area.

One factor that affects climate is latitude. The equator is at zero degrees. The North and South poles are at 90 degrees. Earth curves away from the Sun as latitudes increase. The Sun's rays have to travel farther to reach points directly above and below the equator. As latitude increases, the climate gets colder.

Climate is also affected by Earth's yearly trip around the Sun. Earth is tilted on its axis. (Earth's axis is an imaginary line that runs through Earth's center from pole to pole.) As Earth circles the Sun, sometimes Earth's top half is tilted toward the Sun. At other times, the bottom half is tilted toward the Sun. The half that is closer to the Sun is warmer. This is why the seasons change.

Air movement also affects climate. The hot air at the equator rises, and the cold air at the poles sinks. This makes air currents. These air currents distribute heat across the earth.

Finally, the climate of an area can also be affected by the area's terrain, elevation, and relation to an ocean, lake, or mountain range.

1. **Recognizing Words in Context**

   Find the word *distribute* in the passage. One definition below is closest to the meaning of that word. One definition has the opposite or nearly the opposite meaning. The remaining definition has a completely different meaning. Label the definitions C for *closest*, O for *opposite or nearly opposite*, and D for *different*.

   _____ a. spread out

   _____ b. inform

   _____ c. gather

2. **Distinguishing Fact from Opinion**

   Two of the statements below present *facts,* which can be proved. The other statement is an *opinion*, which expresses someone's thoughts or beliefs. Label the statements F for *fact* and O for *opinion*.

   _____ a. Cooler climates are more comfortable than warmer ones.

   _____ b. Latitude affects climate.

   _____ c. The hot air at the equator rises.

3. Keeping Events in Order

Number the statements below 1, 2, and 3 to show the order in which the events took place.

_____ a. The exchange of hot air and cold air makes air currents.

_____ b. The hot air rises at the equator, and the cold air at the poles sinks.

_____ c. Air currents distribute heat across Earth.

4. Making Correct Inferences

Two of the statements below are correct *inferences,* or reasonable guesses. They are based on information in the passage. The other statement is an incorrect, or faulty, inference. Label the statements C for *correct* inference and F for *faulty* inference.

_____ a. The climate of an area cannot be predicted reliably on the basis of latitude alone.

_____ b. Air movement is the most important factor in determining climate.

_____ c. As one travels away from the equator, the climate becomes cooler.

5. Understanding Main Ideas

One of the statements below expresses the main idea of the passage. One statement is too general, or too broad. The other explains only part of the passage; it is too narrow. Label the statements M for *main idea,* B for *too broad,* and N for *too narrow.*

_____ a. Climate is affected by Earth's yearly trip around the Sun.

_____ b. Climates vary throughout the world.

_____ c. The explanation for climate is complex and involves many factors.

Correct Answers, Part A _____

Correct Answers, Part B _____

Total Correct Answers _____

Life Inside a Medieval Castle

The medieval period lasted about 1,000 years, from the fifth to the fifteenth century. During this time, the great lords of Europe lived in castles. A castle was the center of a local land system managed by a lord. A castle was also a stronghold against enemies. The lord's serfs worked the land in return for protection and a small cottage and land.

The first castles were wooden structures set on high ground and were surrounded by walls. Each had a great hall where people ate their meals and slept. Later castles had stone towers. A water-filled ditch, called a moat, often encircled the castle. Inside, on an upper floor, were the family's bedchambers. The lord and the lady slept in one chamber, and their children shared another. The lord's family had feather mattresses, warm blankets, and furs. The family's personal servants slept on pallets, or bed rolls, on the floor. Others who lived in the castle slept in the towers, and men-at-arms slept near their posts.

Water came from a well near or inside the castle. People bathed in wooden tubs. In warm weather the tub was outside, but in cold weather it was inside, near a fireplace. For toilets, people used chamber pots or a garderobe. A garderobe was a toilet set into a wall, built out from the castle. The waste fell into the moat below.

At sunrise a guard sounded a trumpet, and the lord's family rose and dressed. The maids cleaned the bedchambers and emptied the chamber pots, and the laundress began the day's wash. After everyone had a breakfast of bread and drink, the priest said Mass in the chapel. Then everyone went to his or her work. The lord would see to the castle business while the lady supervised the household servants. These might include cooks, maids, and the spinners and weavers who made everyone's clothes. The lord's children went to a schoolroom, usually in the chapel, to learn lessons from the priest. Afterward, they played. Servants' children worked at castle chores. Pages were taught lessons and hunting. The pages were sons of nobles who lived at the castle from age 7. At age 14, they became squires and were taught by a knight to become warriors.

Everyone gathered in the hall for the main meal of the day. The lord and his family sat at a table on a platform. Others sat on benches at lesser tables.

Reading Time _____

Recalling Facts

1. The medieval period lasted from about the fifth to the _____ century.
   - ❑ a. sixth
   - ❑ b. tenth
   - ❑ c. fifteenth

2. The first castles were
   - ❑ a. wooden structures set on high ground.
   - ❑ b. stone towers.
   - ❑ c. cottages.

3. The water-filled ditch that encircled a castle was called a
   - ❑ a. stronghold.
   - ❑ b. moat.
   - ❑ c. garderobe.

4. The lord and lady of a castle slept in
   - ❑ a. the chapel.
   - ❑ b. the tower.
   - ❑ c. a bedchamber.

5. The main meal of the day was eaten in the
   - ❑ a. hall.
   - ❑ b. kitchen.
   - ❑ c. schoolroom.

Understanding Ideas

6. From reading the passage, one can infer that medieval castles
   - ❑ a. served many needs.
   - ❑ b. were used to house the serfs.
   - ❑ c. served as a kitchen for the village.

7. From reading the passage, one can infer that castles were built on high ground so that
   - ❑ a. they could be better defended from enemies.
   - ❑ b. rainwater would run off into the moat.
   - ❑ c. animals could not get into the castle.

8. From the passage, one can infer that in a castle
   - ❑ a. the knights had the most important jobs.
   - ❑ b. personal servants worked harder than the cooks.
   - ❑ c. many people did different jobs to keep the castle running.

9. In the hall, the lord and lady most likely sat at a higher table
   - ❑ a. so that they could see the other tables.
   - ❑ b. as a way to show that their rank was higher than the others'.
   - ❑ c. so that they could be served first.

10. If a person worked in a castle and slept in the lord's bedchamber, he or she was probably
    - ❑ a. a kitchen servant.
    - ❑ b. a man-at-arms.
    - ❑ c. the lord's or the lady's personal servant.

Food Fit for a King

In a medieval castle, servants prepared three meals a day. Breakfast was usually bread and cheese, eaten at dawn. At the main meal, the lord's family dined on spiced meat, vegetables in sauces, fish, fruit, nuts, and pastries. Those at the lesser tables had some of the same food, but the best foods were only for the lord's table. Supper, at sunset, might be bread, cheese, and meat.

Feasts were held on special days or to honor a visit from the king. A king's visit was a challenge because the lord of the castle had to offer an elaborate feast. He also had to feed the king's party, which could number more than 1,000 people.

The first course might be venison with boiled wheat, boar's head, roasted piglets, and roasted swans. There might be custard, tarts, and a subtlety. A subtlety is fancy food that looks like an object or an animal, perhaps a pastry castle or fruit made of sugar.

The second course might be jellied calves' feet soup, roasted crane, pheasant, heron, peacocks, rabbits, and a fish dish. These also would be served with a subtlety.

A third course might include almond soup, roasted quail, and chicken. Meat in pastry, meat stew, and fruit tarts might also be offered. Sometimes a king's visit would use up all of the castle's food stores and livestock.

1. **Recognizing Words in Context**

   Find the word *elaborate* in the passage. One definition below is closest to the meaning of that word. One definition has the opposite or nearly the opposite meaning. The remaining definition has a completely different meaning. Label the definitions C for *closest,* O for *opposite or nearly opposite,* and D for *different.*

   _____ a. fancy

   _____ b. pitiful

   _____ c. plain

2. **Distinguishing Fact from Opinion**

   Two of the statements below present *facts,* which can be proved. The other statement is an *opinion,* which expresses someone's thoughts or beliefs. Label the statements F for *fact* and O for *opinion.*

   _____ a. Feasts were held when the king visited.

   _____ b. Feasts were served in courses.

   _____ c. Subtleties were a waste of good food.

3. Keeping Events in Order

Number the statements below 1, 2, and 3 to show the order in which the events took place.

_____ a. Supper, at sunset, might be bread, cheese, and meat.

_____ b. Breakfast was eaten at dawn.

_____ c. At the main meal, the lord's family had many foods.

4. Making Correct Inferences

Two of the statements below are correct *inferences,* or reasonable guesses. They are based on information in the passage. The other statement is an incorrect, or faulty, inference. Label the statements C for *correct* inference and F for *faulty* inference.

_____ a. At the main meal, kings and lords ate better than others who lived in the castle.

_____ b. Very plain foods were eaten at a feast.

_____ c. A visit from the king meant a lot of work for the castle's people.

5. Understanding Main Ideas

One of the statements below expresses the main idea of the passage. One statement is too general, or too broad. The other explains only part of the passage; it is too narrow. Label the statements M for *main idea,* B for *too broad,* and N for *too narrow.*

_____ a. In a medieval castle, three meals were served every day; and fancy, multicourse feasts were held on special occasions.

_____ b. The first course of a medieval feast might include venison with boiled wheat.

_____ c. Food was an important part of medieval society.

Correct Answers, Part A _____

Correct Answers, Part B _____

Total Correct Answers _____

Abraham Lincoln and the Gettysburg Address

Abraham Lincoln became president in 1860. At the time, the North's economy was based on industry. The South depended more on crops. The North did not allow slavery. The South used enslaved people to raise its crops. Both the North and the South wanted to force their views on the entire country. Lincoln was against slavery. The South saw him as a threat to its way of life. The South declared its separation from the Union and set up its own government, the Confederate States of America. The Civil War began.

In 1863 troops from both sides fought a huge battle at Gettysburg, Pennsylvania. Thousands of soldiers from each side died. Part of the battlefield became a national cemetery. Officials asked Lincoln to make a dedication speech at the site.

Lincoln's speech took place during one of the darkest times in the nation's history. After three years of war, the country was more divided than ever. People in the Union doubted that it would ever be truly united.

Lincoln's speech is now known as the Gettysburg Address. Its first words are famous: "Fourscore and seven years ago, our fathers brought forth on this continent a new nation: conceived in liberty and dedicated to the proposition that all men are created equal." Lincoln used these words to remind people of the reason for the nation's birth. It was born so that its people could be free. Lincoln called the Civil War a test of the nation's strength. He said that it was fitting for part of the battlefield to be used as a resting place for those who gave their lives. He declared that those who fought there had blessed the ground and that the living must finish the work of winning the war. His words were "We . . . resolve that these dead shall not have died in vain." He ended his speech with "This government of the people—by the people—for the people—shall not perish from the Earth."

Lincoln's speech took only about two minutes. It was direct, heartfelt, and humble. The newspapers printed the speech. It struck a chord in the heart of the Union. His speech gave the Union the resolve to fight on and win the war. His speech is one of the most powerful in U.S. history. The words still have meaning today. They were not just about the Civil War. They tell what the United States stands for—freedom and equal rights for all.

Reading Time _____

Recalling Facts

1. At the time Lincoln became president, the North's economy was based on
   - ❑ a. slavery.
   - ❑ b. industry.
   - ❑ c. crops.

2. The South set up a government called the
   - ❑ a. Union.
   - ❑ b. Confederate States of America.
   - ❑ c. Civil States.

3. The Gettysburg Address begins with the words
   - ❑ a. "Fourscore and seven years ago, our fathers . . . "
   - ❑ b. "These dead shall not have died in vain."
   - ❑ c. "This government of the people—by the people—for the people—shall not perish from the Earth."

4. Lincoln's speech took about _____ minutes.
   - ❑ a. two
   - ❑ b. ten
   - ❑ c. thirty

5. The Gettysburg Address is a
   - ❑ a. Civil War battlefield.
   - ❑ b. national cemetery.
   - ❑ c. well-known and powerful speech.

Understanding Ideas

6. From reading the passage, one can infer that when Lincoln took office the country was
   - ❑ a. peaceful.
   - ❑ b. at war.
   - ❑ c. in a state of conflict.

7. From reading the passage, one can infer that Lincoln most wanted to
   - ❑ a. reunite the Union.
   - ❑ b. destroy the South.
   - ❑ c. keep the country at war.

8. Of the following, Lincoln's speech did not
   - ❑ a. honor those who died in battle.
   - ❑ b. call for a cease-fire.
   - ❑ c. inspire the Union.

9. From the passage, one can infer that Lincoln's speech was
   - ❑ a. a failure.
   - ❑ b. long, with many details.
   - ❑ c. short and powerful.

10. From information in the passage, one can infer that Lincoln
    - ❑ a. wanted to preserve the Union.
    - ❑ b. fought in the battle of Gettysburg.
    - ❑ c. ordered the South to leave the Union.

The Careers of Abraham Lincoln

Before he became president, Abraham Lincoln had a variety of careers. One of his first jobs was as a farmhand in Indiana. He was still in school, reading all the books he could. When he was 19 years old, he took farm produce by flatboat to New Orleans to sell. Two years later, his family moved to Illinois. Lincoln went to work as a store clerk. He took part in a wrestling match and joined a debating group. He continued to read as much as he could.

Then Lincoln became interested in politics. He ran for a seat in the Illinois General Assembly. When he was not elected, he worked as a postmaster. In addition to doing that, he worked as a land surveyor.

Lincoln was 24 years old when he was elected to the Illinois General Assembly. From there he went on to study law. He became a partner in a law firm and later brought cases before the Illinois Supreme Court. In a few years, he was elected to the U.S. House of Representatives.

At age 40, Lincoln left politics to practice law. He gained fame as a lawyer. He also became an inventor and was granted a patent for a device that helped steamboats move through shallow water. At the age of 51, Lincoln was elected president of the United States.

1. Recognizing Words in Context

Find the word *granted* in the passage. One definition below is closest to the meaning of that word. One definition has the opposite or nearly the opposite meaning. The remaining definition has a completely different meaning. Label the definitions C for *closest*, O for *opposite or nearly opposite*, and D for *different*.

_____ a. denied

_____ b. given

_____ c. measured

2. Distinguishing Fact from Opinion

Two of the statements below present *facts*, which can be proved. The other statement is an *opinion*, which expresses someone's thoughts or beliefs. Label the statements F for *fact* and O for *opinion*.

_____ a. Lincoln worked as a store clerk.

_____ b. Lincoln became well known as a lawyer.

_____ c. Lincoln worked too many jobs at the same time.

3. Keeping Events in Order

Number the statements below 1, 2, and 3 to show the order in which the events took place.

_____ a. One of Lincoln's first jobs was as a farmhand in Indiana.

_____ b. At the age of 51, he became president of the United States.

_____ c. Lincoln worked as a post-master and land surveyor.

4. Making Correct Inferences

Two of the statements below are correct *inferences,* or reasonable guesses. They are based on information in the passage. The other statement is an incorrect, or faulty, inference. Label the statements C for *correct* inference and F for *faulty* inference.

_____ a. Lincoln did not like politics.

_____ b. Lincoln had many careers.

_____ c. Lincoln was a smart man with many talents.

5. Understanding Main Ideas

One of the statements below expresses the main idea of the passage. One statement is too general, or too broad. The other explains only part of the passage; it is too narrow. Label the statements M for *main idea*, B for *too broad*, and N for *too narrow*.

_____ a. Lincoln had many talents and many careers.

_____ b. Lincoln took part in a wrestling match.

_____ c. Lincoln was a great man.

Correct Answers, Part A _____

Correct Answers, Part B _____

Total Correct Answers _____

The People of Hawaii

The islands of Hawaii are located in the South Pacific Ocean. People of many different races, cultures, and beliefs live there. The largest groups are Asian people and people from other Pacific islands. These groups get along well with each other. Marriage between people of different races is common.

The earliest Hawaiians came from Polynesia. They came by canoe more than 1,000 years ago. They farmed and fished and lived in small villages. One day in 1778, a ship came from England. The natives were amazed at the white skin of Captain James Cook and his crew. At first they thought the white men were gods. Soon more ships from Europe and North America stopped at the islands. They were on their way to and from the East where the sailors traded goods. They stopped at the islands to pick up food.

The trade ships brought people from many distant places. These people brought their skills and their animals, too. Captain George Vancouver brought cattle from California. The European settlers brought more animals and new kinds of plants. The settlers sold the meat from the cows to whaling ships that came to port. The cows grew in number and ran wild on the islands. They ate and trampled the crops. Ranchers came from Mexico and Spain to herd the cows. One Spaniard, Don Marín, was the first to grow coffee on the islands. Missionaries from New England brought their Christian religions to the islands. They taught the natives to read and write. One trade ship brought Chinese carpenters to the islands. The Germans came and built sugar mills. Other settlers started pineapple plantations. They needed people to work in the fields. Workers came from Puerto Rico, Spain, China, Korea, and Japan. They planned to make money to take back home with them, but many never left. Hawaii became their new home.

The new arrivals also brought diseases with them, which spread to the natives. Many natives died, and some left the islands. As more and more immigrants came, the number of natives decreased.

By 1900 Hawaii had become a U.S. territory. The U.S. military base there came under attack by Japan during World War II. After the war, Hawaii became popular with tourists. Some of these visitors liked the islands so much that they moved there. Since Captain Cook's arrival, people from many lands and the natives have shaped a truly multicultural society.

Reading Time _____

Recalling Facts

1. Hawaii is located in the
   - ❑ a. South Pacific Ocean.
   - ❑ b. East Atlantic Ocean.
   - ❑ c. Antarctic Ocean.

2. The largest groups of people in Hawaii are
   - ❑ a. Spaniards and Mexicans.
   - ❑ b. English and Americans.
   - ❑ c. Asians and people from other Pacific islands.

3. The first ship from the West was captained by
   - ❑ a. James Cook.
   - ❑ b. Don Marín.
   - ❑ c. George Vancouver.

4. The first cattle on the islands were brought from
   - ❑ a. Europe.
   - ❑ b. California.
   - ❑ c. Spain.

5. The first person to grow coffee on the islands was
   - ❑ a. George Vancouver.
   - ❑ b. James Cook.
   - ❑ c. Don Marín.

Understanding Ideas

6. From reading the passage, one can conclude that people from many places settled in Hawaii and
   - ❑ a. kept their cultural traditions without any change.
   - ❑ b. created a new culture by blending traditions.
   - ❑ c. worked hard to fit into the culture of the native Hawaiians.

7. It is likely that immigration to Hawaii began because
   - ❑ a. missionaries wanted to teach Christianity to the natives.
   - ❑ b. the islands had been discovered by trade ships.
   - ❑ c. Americans wanted to put a military base there.

8. It is likely that people came to Hawaii from so many places because
   - ❑ a. they wanted religious freedom.
   - ❑ b. Hawaii is located between the East and the West.
   - ❑ c. they could live and work on a plantation there.

9. From reading the passage, one can conclude that the natives of Hawaii
   - ❑ a. have both benefited and suffered from immigration.
   - ❑ b. outnumber the immigrants.
   - ❑ c. experienced some, but little, change after immigrants arrived.

10. Which of the following sentences tells what the whole passage is about?
    - ❑ a. Hawaii's location made it a good place for trade.
    - ❑ b. Hawaii is a blend of people from many cultures.
    - ❑ c. Hawaii became a U.S. territory in 1900.

The Hula: Ancient and Modern Dance of Hawaii

The earliest residents of Hawaii created a dance called the hula, which means dance. The hula was part of the natives' religion and was danced to honor the gods, especially the goddess Laka. The dancers used arm and hand movements to express prayers that were chanted. They played log drums covered with sharkskin, called *pahu*. Native Hawaiians also used the hula as entertainment. The people danced to tell of births and deaths and the glories of their chiefs. They performed the hula both standing and sitting. Those who sat chanted; those who stood interpreted the chant with gestures. The name of this ancient form of the hula is *kahiko*.

By the 1820s, missionaries had come to the islands. They saw the hula as a pagan rite and banned the natives from dancing it, but a few natives kept dancing the hula in secret. Years later there was a return to some of the old customs. The hula came back in a new form. The dancers added singing, costumes, and new instruments. This modern dance, or *auwana hula,* is playful. It is quite different from the ancient dance.

Now there is new interest in the ancient hula. Dancers who learned it from their elders have kept it alive. There are competitions each year for both forms of the dance.

1. **Recognizing Words in Context**

   Find the word *banned* in the passage. One definition below is closest to the meaning of that word. One definition has the opposite or nearly the opposite meaning. The remaining definition has a completely different meaning. Label the definitions C for *closest,* O for *opposite or nearly opposite,* and D for *different.*

   _____ a. outlawed

   _____ b. allowed

   _____ c. believed

2. **Distinguishing Fact from Opinion**

   Two of the statements below present *facts,* which can be proved. The other statement is an *opinion,* which expresses someone's thoughts or beliefs. Label the statements F for *fact* and O for *opinion.*

   _____ a. The word *hula* means dance.

   _____ b. The ancient form of the hula is called *kahiko.*

   _____ c. Ancient hula is boring compared to the modern form of the dance.

3. Keeping Events in Order

Number the statements below 1, 2, and 3 to show the order in which the events took place.

_____ a. The first people of Hawaii created the hula.

_____ b. Today both forms of the hula are performed.

_____ c. The hula was banned in the 1820s.

4. Making Correct Inferences

Two of the statements below are correct *inferences*, or reasonable guesses. They are based on information in the passage. The other statement is an incorrect, or faulty, inference. Label the statements C for *correct* inference and F for *faulty* inference.

_____ a. The ancient hula is no longer danced in the Hawaiian islands.

_____ b. Missionaries were probably ignorant of the cultural importance of the hula.

_____ c. The new interest in the ancient hula probably is the result of native Hawaiians' pride in their cultural heritage.

5. Understanding Main Ideas

One of the statements below expresses the main idea of the passage. One statement is too general, or too broad. The other explains only part of the passage; it is too narrow. Label the statements M for *main idea*, B for *too broad*, and N for *too narrow*.

_____ a. Two forms of hula, ancient and modern, were created in Hawaii.

_____ b. Log drums were played during the ancient hula.

_____ c. The hula is a Hawaiian dance.

Correct Answers, Part A _____

Correct Answers, Part B _____

Total Correct Answers _____

12   A   Life in Ancient China During the Han Dynasty

The Han Dynasty in China ruled from 206 B.C. to A.D. 220. A dynasty is a line of rulers from the same family that holds power for a long time. Liu Bang was the first ruler of the Han Dynasty. He led an army and took over more and more land. He called himself King of Han, which was one of the states he ruled. Liu followed the teachings of the Chinese thinker Confucius. These teachings stressed love, goodness, and learning. Liu set up a school for children to learn Confucianism. They also learned writing, poetry, and art. A later Han ruler, Wudi, created a civil service examination. People could go to school to study for this test. Those who passed became government officials. Wudi opened the Silk Road. This trade route linked China with other countries. It allowed the Chinese to trade the beautiful silk fabric they made for riches from faraway places.

To the Han people, family included all of the living generations. It also included ancestors who had died and people who had not been born yet. The Han people believed that it was good luck to have five generations living together. The father was the head of the family. He decided what his children would do and whom they married. A woman could be the family head if her husband died. Boys were educated at school, but girls received their education at home.

Most of the people were farmers. They lived in mud houses with thatched roofs. More than one family might live together and work the land. In the North, people grew wheat and millet. Where the land was wet, they grew rice. Farmers traded extra food for other things they needed. They worked from sunup until sundown. They wore plain clothes of rough cloth and straw sandals.

About 10 percent of the people lived in the cities. Cities were laid out in a square with a grid of streets. A wall surrounded each city. One entered or left a city through a gate, watched by guards. People shopped in the marketplace where there was free entertainment. Everyone enjoyed the jugglers, musicians, and acrobats. Rich officials lived in large houses. They had carpets, drapes, art, and fine furniture. Craftsmen, artists, and merchants belonged to guilds. These associations set prices for goods and the times the members worked.

Reading Time _____

Recalling Facts

1. A dynasty is
   - ❑ a. a king and his court.
   - ❑ b. a line of rulers from the same family that holds power for a long time.
   - ❑ c. a thousand years.

2. The first Han ruler was
   - ❑ a. Liu Bang.
   - ❑ b. Confucius.
   - ❑ c. Wudi.

3. The Silk Road is
   - ❑ a. a trade route that linked China with other countries.
   - ❑ b. the road leading to the ruler's palace.
   - ❑ c. the longest river in China.

4. Chinese families were made up of
   - ❑ a. the living generations, the ancestors, and those to come.
   - ❑ b. a husband, wife, and children.
   - ❑ c. three generations.

5. Cities were laid out
   - ❑ a. in a circle.
   - ❑ b. along one long street.
   - ❑ c. in a square.

Understanding Ideas

6. From the passage, one can infer that Liu Bang
   - ❑ a. wanted only to be rich.
   - ❑ b. valued education.
   - ❑ c. put all of his effort into waging war.

7. It is most likely that a government official of the Han Dynasty
   - ❑ a. knew how to read and write.
   - ❑ b. was a member of the ruler's family.
   - ❑ c. was appointed by the ruler.

8. Elderly people in the Han Dynasty probably lived
   - ❑ a. alone in a mud hut.
   - ❑ b. in the city with other old people.
   - ❑ c. with their children and grandchildren.

9. During the Han Dynasty, a farmer
   - ❑ a. had many luxuries.
   - ❑ b. worked long hours.
   - ❑ c. was able to take many vacations.

10. From the passage, one can infer that the Han Dynasty was a time of
    - ❑ a. learning and trade.
    - ❑ b. starvation.
    - ❑ c. confusion and unrest.

12 　 B 　 Papermaking in the Han Dynasty

People had been writing long before the Han Dynasty; centuries earlier, the Egyptians wrote on papyrus, a thin mat of pounded reeds. The word *paper* comes from the word *papyrus*. The ancient Chinese wrote on silk, bamboo, bones, wood, and stones. It was inconvenient to write on these things, so they were not used often.

People first wrote on true paper in China during the Han Dynasty. In about A.D. 105, T'sai Lun, a court official, made paper, in a series of steps, out of fishing nets, bark, rags, and bits of rope.

Step 1: Plants such as bamboo and mulberry bark were soaked in water, which broke them down into single fibers.

Step 2: The fibers, along with hemp and rag fibers, were put into a large vat of water.

Step 3: A fine screen was used to collect a thin layer, or sheet, of fibers.

Step 4: The water was pressed out of the sheet. This formed the sheet into what we call paper.

Step 5: The sheets were hung up and smoothed out.

Step 6: The sheets were dried.

T'sai Lun's paper was thin and smooth and easy to write on. The emperor was so pleased that he called the paper *T'sai Ko-Shij*, which means "Distinguished T'sai's Paper."

1. **Recognizing Words in Context**

   Find the word *smoothed* in the passage. One definition below is closest to the meaning of that word. One definition has the opposite or nearly the opposite meaning. The remaining definition has a completely different meaning. Label the definitions C for *closest*, O for *opposite or nearly opposite*, and D for *different*.

   _____ a. flattened

   _____ b. heavy

   _____ c. crumpled

2. **Distinguishing Fact from Opinion**

   Two of the statements below present *facts*, which can be proved. The other statement is an *opinion*, which expresses someone's thoughts or beliefs. Label the statements F for *fact* and O for *opinion*.

   _____ a. In about A.D. 105, T'sai Lun made true paper.

   _____ b. The emperor called Lun's paper T'sai Ko-Shij.

   _____ c. Silk is easier to write on than papyrus.

3. Keeping Events in Order

Number the statements below 1, 2, and 3 to show the order in which the events took place.

_____ a. The sheets were hung up and smoothed out.

_____ b. A screen was used to collect a thin layer, or sheet, of fibers.

_____ c. The plant fibers and hemp and rag fibers were put into a vat of water.

4. Making Correct Inferences

Two of the statements below are correct *inferences,* or reasonable guesses. They are based on information in the passage. The other statement is an incorrect, or faulty, inference. Label the statements C for *correct* inference and F for *faulty* inference.

_____ a. T'sai Lun used papyrus to invent paper.

_____ b. The steps of the papermaking process must be done in the correct order.

_____ c. T'sai Lun was an inventor.

5. Understanding Main Ideas

One of the statements below expresses the main idea of the passage. One statement is too general, or too broad. The other explains only part of the passage; it is too narrow. Label the statements M for *main idea,* B for *too broad,* and N for *too narrow.*

_____ a. In step 6, the sheets were dried.

_____ b. The making of paper has changed a great deal over many centuries.

_____ c. T'sai Lun went through a series of steps to make paper.

Correct Answers, Part A _____

Correct Answers, Part B _____

Total Correct Answers _____

The Underground Railroad

Before the Civil War, many people in southern states used enslaved African Americans for labor. These African Americans were brought to the United States from Africa against their will. They could be bought and sold. They could be beaten or mistreated, as the slaveholder wished. Abolitionists were people who acted against slavery.

By about 1800, a secret group of people were helping enslaved African Americans to escape. They gave runaways hiding places. These abolitionists gave the runaways clothes and food and guided them to the North, where they helped the runaways find jobs. People used railroad terms to describe the secret network. They called it the Underground Railroad. The places where runaways rested and ate were called "stations" or "depots." A "conductor" was a person who moved passengers (runaways) from one place to the next. Those who gave money to help the runaways were called "stockholders."

Many African Americans chose to run to freedom. One of these was Harriet Tubman. She lived on a plantation in Maryland. When she learned that she was to be sold, she ran away. Some Quakers and some free African Americans helped her. She safely reached Philadelphia. There she found a job and saved her money. Tubman went back to the South many times to help others escape. She became one of the most famous conductors of the Underground Railroad. Tubman used many tricks to help runaways get away. Sometimes she used a slaveholder's horse and buggy for the first part of the trip. Runaways would leave on a Saturday night. That way they would not be reported missing in the newspapers until Monday. Tubman was never caught. She never lost a passenger.

In 1850 the Fugitive Slave Bill became law. The new law permitted slaveholders to hunt and capture runaways in any state. This meant that the North was no longer safe. The "conductors" began taking runaways to Canada.

Slaveholders hired hunters to find the runaways and bring them back. Captured runaways were punished. Sometimes they were killed. Posters described the runaways and offered rewards.

Runaways traveled at night. To keep moving north, they followed the North Star. A popular song was "Follow the Drinking Gourd." The drinking gourd referred to the star formation called the Little Dipper. The North Star was part of this formation. A runaway might travel 10 or 20 miles each night. A lantern on a hitching post was one mark of a friendly house.

Reading Time _____

Recalling Facts

1. People who acted against slavery were called
   - ❑ a. abolitionists.
   - ❑ b. runaways.
   - ❑ c. hunters.

2. A person who guided runaways from one place to the next was called a
   - ❑ a. stockholder.
   - ❑ b. passenger.
   - ❑ c. conductor.

3. Harriet Tubman was
   - ❑ a. a runaway who helped many others to escape.
   - ❑ b. a runaway slave who was caught and punished.
   - ❑ c. a Quaker.

4. The Fugitive Slave Bill permitted slaveholders to
   - ❑ a. capture runaways in any state.
   - ❑ b. capture runaway slaves in the South.
   - ❑ c. follow slaves into Canada.

5. The drinking gourd referred to
   - ❑ a. the Underground Railroad.
   - ❑ b. the Little Dipper.
   - ❑ c. a place to find water.

Understanding Ideas

6. From the passage, one can infer that members of the Underground Railroad
   - ❑ a. were willing to break the law.
   - ❑ b. did not act in secret.
   - ❑ c. bragged about what they did.

7. Harriet Tubman probably never got caught or lost a passenger because she
   - ❑ a. made only a few trips to rescue African Americans.
   - ❑ b. used clever schemes.
   - ❑ c. was very lucky.

8. Which of the following sentences tells what the whole passage is about?
   - ❑ a. Harriet Tubman escaped slavery.
   - ❑ b. Enslaved African Americans ran away at night.
   - ❑ c. The Underground Railroad was a network that helped runaways to escape to freedom.

9. One can infer that after the Fugitive Slave Bill was passed,
   - ❑ a. Canada was the closest safe place for fugitives.
   - ❑ b. there were no more jobs in the North for runaways.
   - ❑ c. the conductors were afraid to continue helping runaways.

10. After a runaway left the plantation, it is most likely that he or she would
    - ❑ a. hide on a nearby plantation.
    - ❑ b. look for a lantern on a hitching post.
    - ❑ c. steal a horse and buggy.

13   B   Juneteenth

For African Americans, Juneteenth is a celebration of freedom. It marks the day the last African Americans in the country became free. On June 19, 1865, after the Civil War ended, Union soldiers went to Texas. They told the people that the war was over and announced that the African Americans were free. Texas African Americans were the last to gain freedom. In January of 1863, Lincoln had signed the Emancipation Proclamation. This law freed African Americans in states fighting the Union. Texas was part of the South. However, Union soldiers could not get into Texas during the war. Only after the war ended did African Americans in Texas learn that they were free.

African Americans celebrated their freedom. Some threw off their ragged clothes. They dressed as free men. They prayed and held feasts in their churches. They called the day Juneteenth. This is because the date was June 19th. In the years that followed, barbecues and baseball games took place on Juneteenth. Those who had been enslaved told about the first day of freedom.

Education has always been a big part of Juneteenth. In 1980 it became a state holiday in Texas. Now Juneteenth is celebrated in many states.

1. **Recognizing Words in Context**

   Find the word *ragged* in the passage. One definition below is closest to the meaning of that word. One definition has the opposite or nearly the opposite meaning. The remaining definition has a completely different meaning. Label the definitions C for *closest,* O for *opposite or nearly opposite,* and D for *different.*

   _____ a. new

   _____ b. tattered

   _____ c. colorful

2. **Distinguishing Fact from Opinion**

   Two of the statements below present *facts,* which can be proved. The other statement is an *opinion,* which expresses someone's thoughts or beliefs. Label the statements F for *fact* and O for *opinion.*

   _____ a. Juneteenth marks the day that the last African Americans were set free.

   _____ b. It is fun to play baseball on Juneteenth and be a part of the other activities.

   _____ c. In 1863 President Lincoln signed the Emancipation Proclamation.

3. Keeping Events in Order

Number the statements below 1, 2, and 3 to show the order in which the events took place.

_____ a. Union soldiers went to Texas.

_____ b. Slaves in Texas celebrated their freedom.

_____ c. Juneteenth is celebrated in many states.

4. Making Correct Inferences

Two of the statements below are correct *inferences,* or reasonable guesses. They are based on information in the passage. The other statement is an incorrect, or faulty, inference. Label the statements C for *correct* inference and F for *faulty* inference.

_____ a. Juneteenth reminds Americans that freedom does not come easily.

_____ b. The ongoing war prevented African Americans in Texas from learning about their freedom before 1865.

_____ c. African Americans in Texas were bitter about its taking two years for them to learn of their freedom.

5. Understanding Main Ideas

One of the statements below expresses the main idea of the passage. One statement is too general, or too broad. The other explains only part of the passage; it is too narrow. Label the statements M for *main idea,* B for *too broad,* and N for *too narrow.*

_____ a. Juneteenth, which commemorates the emancipation of the last African Americans, is a celebration of freedom.

_____ b. The Union victory in the Civil War led to many social changes.

_____ c. On June 19, 1865, Union soldiers went to Texas.

Correct Answers, Part A _____

Correct Answers, Part B _____

Total Correct Answers _____

Ferdinand Magellan, World Explorer

In 1517 Ferdinand Magellan went to see the king of Spain to ask for ships and men for a voyage to the East Indies. He wanted to travel to the East by sailing west. At that time, no one knew that this was possible. Magellan knew that he had to convince the king that his plan was a good one.

Magellan was from Portugal and had grown up in its royal court. He studied navigation, which inspired him to explore. As a young man, he went to India, and later he helped conquer a kingdom in Southeast Asia. Then he explored the islands of the East Indies as far east as the Moluccas, or Spice Islands. He later went to Morocco and fought against the Moors. After returning to Portugal, he asked his king for ships to explore a western route to the Moluccas. He thought that he might find a passage through South America. When the king refused his request, Magellan went to Spain.

Magellan told the king of Spain that a western route to the Moluccas would allow Spain to join the spice trade. Portugal already controlled the eastern route to the islands. Spices from the islands sold for a large amount of money in Europe.

In 1519 Magellan left Spain with five ships, crossing the Atlantic to the coast of South America. While exploring the coast, one ship was lost, but the rest continued south. Magellan found some narrow straits, or channels, which are now called the Straits of Magellan. One ship deserted and returned to Spain, but Magellan sailed on through the dangerous passages. To the south was a harsh land. The explorers could see fires on the shore. Magellan named the land Tierra del Fuego, meaning "land of fire."

After three weeks, the ships came to an ocean. The ocean was calm. Magellan named it Pacific ("peaceful"). As the ships sailed across the ocean, the food and water ran out. The crew had to eat leather, sawdust, and rats. Many became sick and died. Finally, they reached the Philippines. Natives on the Island of Cebu murdered Magellan. There were only enough men left to sail two ships. Finally, the ships reached the Moluccas. The men wanted to go home the way they had come, but the wind drove them west. When they arrived in Spain, they had sailed around the world. Just one ship with a crew of 19 returned to Spain.

Reading Time _____

Recalling Facts

1. Magellan wanted the king of Spain to give him
   - ❑ a. spices to sell to Portugal.
   - ❑ b. ships and men for a voyage to the East Indies.
   - ❑ c. ships for a journey to India.

2. Magellan was originally from
   - ❑ a. Portugal.
   - ❑ b. Spain.
   - ❑ c. Morocco.

3. The passage that Magellan took through South America to the Pacific Ocean is now called
   - ❑ a. Tierra del Fuego.
   - ❑ b. the Straits of Magellan.
   - ❑ c. the Moluccas.

4. Magellan named the ocean beyond the straits the Pacific because the water was
   - ❑ a. rough.
   - ❑ b. cold.
   - ❑ c. calm.

5. Of the five ships that set out on the journey, how many traveled all the way around the world?
   - ❑ a. one
   - ❑ b. two
   - ❑ c. three

Understanding Ideas

6. The main reason Magellan wanted to find a passage through South America was that he
   - ❑ a. wanted to sell the spices he would bring back.
   - ❑ b. was an explorer and wanted to make a new discovery.
   - ❑ c. was angry with the king of Portugal.

7. The king of Spain had to be convinced to give Magellan ships because
   - ❑ a. there was no known western route to the East.
   - ❑ b. Spain did not have many ships.
   - ❑ c. the king was not interested in the spice trade.

8. The ship that deserted at the straits did so because
   - ❑ a. the food and water supply was low.
   - ❑ b. the straits were dangerous.
   - ❑ c. the men were homesick for Spain.

9. The Spice Islands are
   - ❑ a. south of Spain.
   - ❑ b. east of Spain.
   - ❑ c. north of Spain.

10. From reading the passage, one can conclude that Magellan was the first European explorer to
    - ❑ a. cross the Atlantic.
    - ❑ b. visit the Moluccas.
    - ❑ c. lead an expedition to sail around the world.

Portugal: A Seafaring Country

The fifteenth century was a time of great discovery in Europe. The city of Venice was rich and powerful. Part of its wealth came from selling spices to the rest of Europe. The spices came from islands in the Far East. Other countries wanted to grow and prosper from the spice trade. There was a race to find and conquer the islands where the spices came from, and Portugal led the race.

Portugal is located on the Atlantic Ocean, surrounded by Spain on the north, east, and south. Scientists in Portugal had perfected the tools needed to navigate the seas. If the country wanted to build an empire, it would have to be by sea.

Prince Henry of Portugal was known as "the navigator." He started a school to train sailors and sent out ships to find new trade routes. His sailors explored the coast of Africa and sailed as far as the Canary Islands.

Prince Henry died in 1460. Following his death, Bartolomeu Dias sailed to the tip of Africa, known as the Cape of Good Hope. For the first time, people saw that it was possible to sail around Africa. Later Vasco da Gama sailed all the way to India. Portugal had won the spice race. These explorers conquered the East Indies and ruled over the spice trade for many years.

1. **Recognizing Words in Context**

   Find the word *prosper* in the passage. One definition below is closest to the meaning of that word. One definition has the opposite or nearly the opposite meaning. The remaining definition has a completely different meaning. Label the definitions C for *closest,* O for *opposite or nearly opposite,* and D for *different.*

   _____ a. survive

   _____ b. succeed

   _____ c. fail

2. **Distinguishing Fact from Opinion**

   Two of the statements below present *facts,* which can be proved. The other statement is an *opinion,* which expresses someone's thoughts or beliefs. Label the statements F for *fact* and O for *opinion.*

   _____ a. Prince Henry sent out ships to find new trade routes.

   _____ b. Portugal is on the Atlantic Ocean.

   _____ c. Portuguese sailors were the best sailors in Europe.

3. Keeping Events in Order

Number the statements below 1, 2, and 3 to show the order in which the events took place.

_____ a. Vasco da Gama reached India.

_____ b. Prince Henry died in 1460.

_____ c. Bartolomeu Dias sailed to the tip of Africa.

4. Making Correct Inferences

Two of the statements below are correct *inferences,* or reasonable guesses. They are based on information in the passage. The other statement is an incorrect, or faulty, inference. Label the statements C for *correct* inference and F for *faulty* inference.

_____ a. The Portuguese knew a great deal about sailing.

_____ b. Portuguese explorers made many important discoveries.

_____ c. The Portuguese were the only people in Europe making important discoveries during the fifteenth century.

5. Understanding Main Ideas

One of the statements below expresses the main idea of the passage. One statement is too general, or too broad. The other explains only part of the passage; it is too narrow. Label the statements M for *main idea,* B for *too broad,* and N for *too narrow.*

_____ a. Prince Henry started a school to train sailors.

_____ b. In the fifteenth century, Portugal led the race to conquer the islands of the Far East.

_____ c. Portugal was a seafaring nation.

Correct Answers, Part A _____

Correct Answers, Part B _____

Total Correct Answers _____

Ancient Rock Art in the American Southwest

Rock art is the name given to images scratched or drawn on rock by ancient peoples. In the American Southwest, rock art can be seen on the walls of caves, canyons, and mountains. Many of these sites are in the Four Corners region, where the states of Arizona, Colorado, Utah, and New Mexico meet. More than 7,000 rock art sites have been found just in Utah, where the region's dry desert air has helped to preserve the art.

There are three forms of rock art. The first is petroglyphs, which are pictures carved, pecked, or scratched into the surface of rock. A sharp stone, such as flint, may have been used as a scratching tool. A heavy stone may have been used to pound the sharp stone into the surface. The second form of rock art is pictographs, which are images painted on the rock. The paint was made from colorful natural pigments such as those found in plants, trees, and minerals. The artists applied paint with fingers, brushes made from hair or plant fibers, or hollow bird bones. A third kind of rock art is geoglyphs, which are designs made in the desert floor by scraping away stones.

Some rock art shows stick figures, faces, hands, animals, and trees. Other images are symbols such as zigzag lines, dots, circles, and spirals. Some scientists think these symbols marked the location of water or good hunting grounds. Some think the symbols were put there during religious rites. Others think the symbols tracked the movement of planets and stars. Still others believe that they are just doodles without meaning.

Some rock art may be a form of writing. Large scenes stretch across the vast faces of cliffs. Some scenes seem to tell a story. A hunting scene may contain animals and people with bows and arrows. A scene with many people holding hands could stand for friendship. Rock art in caves may have been a way to decorate the artist's home.

Some rock art in the Southwest is about 200 years old. Other rock art may be 10,000 years old. Archaeologists think ancient Native Americans called the Anasazi created the older works. They lived in caves or built houses of adobe. Adobe is sun-dried brick made from clay and straw. Some villages were built into nooks in the cliffs. The Anasazi were farmers. They were the ancestors of today's Pueblo people. The Pueblo believed the rock art to be sacred.

Reading Time _____

Recalling Facts

1. Rock art is
   - ❑ a. images scratched or drawn on rock by people.
   - ❑ b. brightly colored stones found in the desert.
   - ❑ c. unusual rock formations found in caves.

2. Four Corners is
   - ❑ a. an area in Colorado with a cave in each corner.
   - ❑ b. the place where the states of Arizona, Colorado, Utah, and New Mexico meet.
   - ❑ c. the area along the border of Mexico and the United States.

3. Petroglyphs are
   - ❑ a. sharp stones, such as flint.
   - ❑ b. images painted on rock.
   - ❑ c. images that are carved, pecked, or scratched into the surface of rock.

4. Designs cut in the desert floor are called
   - ❑ a. doodles.
   - ❑ b. geoglyphs.
   - ❑ c. spirals.

5. The most ancient rock art of the Southwest is thought to have been created by
   - ❑ a. the Anasazi.
   - ❑ b. today's Pueblo people.
   - ❑ c. European explorers.

Understanding Ideas

6. From the passage, one can infer that rock art
   - ❑ a. is mostly geometric symbols.
   - ❑ b. includes many kinds of images and scenes.
   - ❑ c. includes images of people but not animals.

7. If, while walking in the desert, one saw a symbol on the desert floor, it would probably be a
   - ❑ a. geoglyph.
   - ❑ b. petroglyph.
   - ❑ c. pictograph.

8. From the passage, one can infer that
   - ❑ a. the main purpose of rock art was to keep track of the planets and stars.
   - ❑ b. rock art is useless doodles.
   - ❑ c. rock art may have had many different uses.

9. Compared with a petroglyph, a pictograph would be
   - ❑ a. larger.
   - ❑ b. more colorful.
   - ❑ c. found in a cave.

10. Which of the following sentences tells what the whole passage is about?
   - ❑ a. Rock art is a form of writing.
   - ❑ b. Ancient rock art was created during religious rites.
   - ❑ c. The rock art of the Southwest includes many images that were created by native people.

Rock Art Tour Do's and Don'ts

Here are some do's and don'ts to follow when on a rock art trip. Following these rules will help protect the environment and the ancient rock art.

When setting out, do stay on used and clearly marked trails. The desert has cryptobiotic soil, which looks like lumpy black crusts. It consists of algae, moss, and bacteria, which keep wind and water from carrying away the desert soil. Avoid walking on this living crust. Do camp where others have camped and place tents on bare soil.

Don't build fires against canyon walls; smoke from fires can damage rock art.

While looking for rock art, do keep an eye out for ruins but do not disturb them: they are fragile and crumbling remains of the ancient artists' homes. They can help scientists learn more about the people.

When viewing rock art, don't touch it: human skin may leave traces of oil on the rock. The oil can make it difficult for scientists to run tests on the art to find out its age. Don't trace over the art with chalk to make it photograph better, and don't climb canyon walls for a closer view. Any contact can damage it.

Do enjoy seeing the rock art and do sketch or photograph it to share this amazing art with others.

1. Recognizing Words in Context

Find the word *fragile* in the passage. One definition below is closest to the meaning of that word. One definition has the opposite or nearly the opposite meaning. The remaining definition has a completely different meaning. Label the definitions C for *closest*, O for *opposite or nearly opposite*, and D for *different*.

_____ a. strong

_____ b. easily damaged

_____ c. evil

2. Distinguishing Fact from Opinion

Two of the statements below present *facts*, which can be proved. The other statement is an *opinion*, which expresses someone's thoughts or beliefs. Label the statements F for *fact* and O for *opinion*.

_____ a. Viewing rock art is an enjoyable way to spend a vacation.

_____ b. The desert has cryptobiotic soil.

_____ c. Human skin may leave traces of oil on rock art.

3. **Keeping Events in Order**

Number the statements below 1, 2, and 3 to show the order in which the events took place.

_____ a. Observe carefully to find ruins.

_____ b. When you find rock art, look at it but don't touch it.

_____ c. Be sure to begin your hike on a clearly marked trail.

4. **Making Correct Inferences**

Two of the statements below are correct *inferences*, or reasonable guesses. They are based on information in the passage. The other statement is an incorrect, or faulty, inference. Label the statements C for *correct* inference and F for *faulty* inference.

_____ a. Rock art should never be photographed.

_____ b. Ancient rock art should be preserved.

_____ c. The desert environment is easily disturbed.

5. **Understanding Main Ideas**

One of the statements below expresses the main idea of the passage. One statement is too general, or too broad. The other explains only part of the passage; it is too narrow. Label the statements M for *main idea*, B for *too broad*, and N for *too narrow*.

_____ a. Following some do's and don'ts on a rock art tour can help protect the environment and the rock art.

_____ b. It is important not to build fires against canyon walls.

_____ c. There are do's and don'ts when hiking in the desert.

Correct Answers, Part A _____

Correct Answers, Part B _____

Total Correct Answers _____

Through the years, many devices have brought heat into people's homes. Colonists in New England burned wood in a fireplace, which was built into an outside wall of the kitchen. Wood burned on a grate on the hearth, the fireplace floor. Smoke and fumes went up the chimney, and so did much of the heat.

The iron-box stove solved this problem. This stove was an enclosed iron box that stood in the middle of a room. Cold air entered through a pipe called a duct. A fire warmed the air, which passed through vents into the room. Smoke went outside through a pipe called a flue. All of the stove's surfaces gave off heat, even after the fire went out. Stoves used less wood and gave more heat than a fireplace, but they left parts of a building cold.

In the 1800s, a new method of heating, called central heating, came into use. It uses one furnace to heat a whole building. Some of the first systems used steam heat. A fire heated water in a boiler, which turned the water into steam. The steam traveled through pipes to radiators in the rooms. A radiator is a series of iron tubes set in a base. The tubes provide enough hot surface to heat the room's air. Some central systems used hot water. A gravity system used warm air. This system worked on the principle that warm air rises and cold air sinks. Heated air from the furnace rose up ducts and into the rooms through grates called registers near the ceiling. The warm air entered the room and, as it cooled, sank. Registers in the floor returned the air to the basement. In about 1910, electric fans were added to push the warm air through the ducts. This is called a forced-air system.

In the early 1900s, most furnaces burned coal, which people shoveled into the furnace several times a day. Eventually, the electric coal stoker and the thermostat took over this job. A thermostat senses changes in the temperature and throws a switch when a room cools. The switch turns on a motor in the stoker, and the stoker feeds coal into the furnace.

During World War I, there was a coal shortage, and oil and natural gas were used as furnace fuels. Today oil and natural gas are still the most commonly used furnace fuels.

Reading Time _____

Recalling Facts

1. Colonists in New England burned _____ in a fireplace to heat their homes.
   - ❑ a. natural gas
   - ❑ b. oil
   - ❑ c. wood

2. A hearth is a
   - ❑ a. fireplace floor.
   - ❑ b. heat register.
   - ❑ c. furnace.

3. An iron-box stove was
   - ❑ a. a kind of boiler.
   - ❑ b. an enclosed iron box that stood in the middle of a room.
   - ❑ c. a forced-air furnace.

4. A gravity heating system heats with
   - ❑ a. warm air.
   - ❑ b. steam.
   - ❑ c. hot water.

5. An electric stoker
   - ❑ a. feeds coal into a furnace.
   - ❑ b. senses changes in the temperature in a room.
   - ❑ c. uses water to heat the air.

Understanding Ideas

6. The iron-box stove probably heated better than a fireplace because
   - ❑ a. it stood in the middle of the room.
   - ❑ b. the smoke went out a flue.
   - ❑ c. it burned less wood.

7. A furnace with a boiler attached is probably part of a _____ system.
   - ❑ a. hot-air
   - ❑ b. hot-water
   - ❑ c. steam-heat

8. From the passage, one can infer that
   - ❑ a. fireplaces were an improvement over iron-box stoves.
   - ❑ b. hot-water heating systems heated better than warm-air systems.
   - ❑ c. different kinds of central heating systems were being used at the same time at one point in U.S. history.

9. Of the following, the one that most evenly heats a house is
   - ❑ a. a central heating system.
   - ❑ b. a fireplace.
   - ❑ c. an iron-box stove.

10. Which of the following sentences tells what the whole passage is about?
    - ❑ a. Wood is the most important fuel in U.S. history.
    - ❑ b. Heating systems have become easier to use and more efficient over the years.
    - ❑ c. The iron-box stove heated better than a fireplace.

Solar heating is a heating method used today in parts of the country that have many hours of direct sunlight. Solar heating uses the Sun's energy. First, a collector captures the Sun's heat. A collector can be a box or frame or a whole room. It has a clear cover, usually glass, that lets sunshine in. Then the Sun's rays hit an absorber, which may be a dark metal sheet, rocks, or bricks painted black, or a tray of water. The absorber soaks up the Sun's rays and gets hot. The collector is insulated, which means that it is enclosed in some material to keep the heat from escaping back outside.

Finally, heat from the collector moves to where it is needed. With active solar heat, fans or pumps move heated air from the collector. Sometimes heat moves naturally to where it is needed. This is called passive solar heat. One example is a sun space—a room with a lot of glass in it to let in sunlight. Stone walls and floors absorb the heat during the day and release it at night.

Solar heat does not rely on fuel such as coal or natural gas; therefore, it does not deplete these natural energy sources. Because no fuel is burned, there is neither smoke nor exhaust fumes to pollute the air.

1. **Recognizing Words in Context**

   Find the word *deplete* in the passage. One definition below is closest to the meaning of that word. One definition has the opposite or nearly the opposite meaning. The remaining definition has a completely different meaning. Label the definitions C for *closest*, O for *opposite or nearly opposite*, and D for *different*.

   _____ a. use up

   _____ b. fill up

   _____ c. walk up

2. **Distinguishing Fact from Opinion**

   Two of the statements below present *facts*, which can be proved. The other statement is an *opinion*, which expresses someone's thoughts or beliefs. Label the statements F for *fact* and O for *opinion*.

   _____ a. Every house should have a sun space.

   _____ b. In solar heating, the Sun's heat is captured by a collector.

   _____ c. The absorber soaks up the Sun's rays and gets hot.

3. Keeping Events in Order

Number the statements below 1, 2, and 3 to show the order in which the events took place.

_____ a. The Sun's heat is captured by a collector.

_____ b. Heat from the collector is moved to where it is needed in the house.

_____ c. The Sun's rays hit an absorber.

4. Making Correct Inferences

Two of the statements below are correct *inferences,* or reasonable guesses. They are based on information in the passage. The other statement is an incorrect, or faulty, inference. Label the statements C for *correct* inference and F for *faulty* inference.

_____ a. Solar heat works better in areas that have many more sunny days than cloudy ones.

_____ b. Passive solar heat requires less energy than active solar heat.

_____ c. Solar heat will become the only heating method used over the next twenty years.

5. Understanding Main Ideas

One of the statements below expresses the main idea of the passage. One statement is too general, or too broad. The other explains only part of the passage; it is too narrow. Label the statements M for *main idea,* B for *too broad,* and N for *too narrow.*

_____ a. Solar heat, which uses a collector to absorb the sun's heat, is a clean and efficient way to heat a building.

_____ b. Passive solar heat is heat that moves naturally to where it is needed.

_____ c. Solar energy, coal, or natural gas can be used to heat homes.

Correct Answers, Part A _____

Correct Answers, Part B _____

Total Correct Answers _____

Bartering Throughout History

Bartering is the exchange of goods or services without the use of money. The trading can be direct; for example, trading baseball cards with a friend is bartering. The trading also can be indirect. A farmer who has milk needs new shoes, and the shoemaker wants nails. The farmer has to trade his milk to get nails; then he can trade the nails for the shoes.

In ancient times, the marketplace was in the center of the town, where people bartered for what they needed. By A.D. 100, trade routes linked Europe, Asia, and Africa. The west coast of Africa traded gold for salt from the Sahara Desert. The desert traders used camels to carry gold and salt north. There the goods crossed the Mediterranean Sea to Europe. This trade route is often called the Gold-and-Salt Route. The so-called Silk Road led from China to the Middle East, Russia, and Europe. People traded silk, jade, and paper from China for gold, grapes, and wool rugs from the West. What is called the Spice Route was a water route from the Spice Islands in the East to Europe. Nutmeg, cloves, and cinnamon were valued in Europe. Barter was the reason Columbus found America: he was looking for a new route to the Spice Islands.

Native Americans in the New World had a barter network. Nations in the Northwest had red flint from the South, and Natives of the Great Lakes had stone from the West. Traders moved food, pottery, blankets, metal, stone, and baskets from nation to nation. Silent barter was used when a group wanted to trade with an enemy. They left goods at a certain place, and the enemy later picked up the goods and left behind other goods. Some native groups had a form of barter called the bride price. A young man who wished to marry gave goods to the bride's father. The bride price might include horses, deerskins, copper, or beads.

The colonists bartered for the island of Manhattan. They probably exchanged cloth, kettles, axes, hoes, drilling tools, and wampum (strings of shells used as money) for the land.

Today one might barter by taking a turn driving a carpool in return for riding another time. There are bartering Web sites and clubs. In a club, one gives the group something and earns credits that can be used to "buy" from others in the club.

Reading Time _____

Recalling Facts

1. Bartering is
   - ❑ a. selling something to get the money to buy something else.
   - ❑ b. trading money for goods.
   - ❑ c. trading goods or services without the use of money.

2. The trade route across the Sahara Desert was called
   - ❑ a. the Silk Road.
   - ❑ b. the Gold-and-Salt Route.
   - ❑ c. the Spice Route.

3. Silent barter was used when
   - ❑ a. the marketplace was closed.
   - ❑ b. traders did not understand each other's languages.
   - ❑ c. a native nation wanted to trade with an enemy.

4. When Columbus found America, he was really looking for
   - ❑ a. salt.
   - ❑ b. a new route to the Spice Islands.
   - ❑ c. the coast of Africa.

5. The colonists bartered with the Native Americans for
   - ❑ a. the island of Manhattan.
   - ❑ b. silk, jade, and paper.
   - ❑ c. spices.

Understanding Ideas

6. From reading the passage, one can infer that
   - ❑ a. bartering has encouraged contact between different peoples.
   - ❑ b. different nations have not had contact with each other until modern times.
   - ❑ c. bartering has not been a good use of time.

7. An ancient trader carrying cinnamon to Europe would probably be traveling by
   - ❑ a. camel.
   - ❑ b. ship.
   - ❑ c. wagon.

8. A dentist whose water pipe is dripping could barter directly with
   - ❑ a. a dog trainer who needs toothpaste.
   - ❑ b. a plumber who has a toothache.
   - ❑ c. a painter who has a large van.

9. Of the following, _____ is *not* a kind of bartering.
   - ❑ a. mowing the music teacher's lawn in return for piano lessons
   - ❑ b. buying lunch for a friend
   - ❑ c. giving someone a sandwich in exchange for a bagel

10. Which of the following sentences tells what the whole passage is about?
    - ❑ a. The Silk Road led from China to the Middle East.
    - ❑ b. The Native Americans had a barter network.
    - ❑ c. People throughout history have used bartering to obtain what they needed and wanted.

A potlatch is a gathering of Native Americans of the Northwest, at which the host gives gifts to the guests. A potlatch may last several days. It is a time to feast, barter, tell tall tales, dance, and hold weddings. Potlatch ceremonies have been held along the West Coast since about 1800. In the early days, guest nations came to trade furs for sea salt, dried fish, dried seaweed, and dried clams. The host gave away much of his family's wealth. The more wealth a host gave away, the greater the esteem in which he was held. A chief might give away so much that the family became poor but would become wealthy again when the family attended a future potlatch.

Today Northwest native groups still hold potlatches. Planning for a potlatch can take months. The host sends out invitations well ahead of time. Then the host family or nation works to prepare food and gifts. When guests arrive, they feast and dance. Trained dancers wear special masks. Some groups use transformation masks. These are masks that open to show a different mask. For example, an animal mask could open to reveal an ancestor mask. Together the mask and dance tell a story.

1. **Recognizing Words in Context**

   Find the word *esteem* in the passage. One definition below is closest to the meaning of that word. One definition has the opposite or nearly the opposite meaning. The remaining definition has a completely different meaning. Label the definitions C for *closest*, O for *opposite or nearly opposite*, and D for *different*.

   _____ a. high regard

   _____ b. disrespect

   _____ c. flaw

2. **Distinguishing Fact from Opinion**

   Two of the statements below present *facts*, which can be proved. The other statement is an *opinion*, which expresses someone's thoughts or beliefs. Label the statements F for *fact* and O for *opinion*.

   _____ a. Potlatch ceremonies have been held since about 1800.

   _____ b. The host of a potlatch is only showing off.

   _____ c. A transformation mask is one that opens to show another mask.

3. Keeping Events in Order

Number the statements below 1, 2, and 3 to show the order in which the events took place.

_____ a. The host family works to prepare food and gifts.

_____ b. Invitations are sent out.

_____ c. When the guests arrive, there is feasting and dancing.

4. Making Correct Inferences

Two of the statements below are correct *inferences,* or reasonable guesses. They are based on information in the passage. The other statement is an incorrect, or faulty, inference. Label the statements C for *correct* inference and F for *faulty* inference.

_____ a. The potlatch ceremony serves many purposes for the Northwest native groups.

_____ b. Keeping the potlatch tradition is important to Northwest natives today.

_____ c. Guests at a potlatch party bring many gifts to the host.

5. Understanding Main Ideas

One of the statements below expresses the main idea of the passage. One statement is too general, or too broad. The other explains only part of the passage; it is too narrow. Label the statements M for *main idea*, B for *too broad*, and N for *too narrow.*

_____ a. The potlatch is a traditional ceremony of the Northwest Native Americans.

_____ b. Some tribes use transformation masks for potlatch ceremonies.

_____ c. Traditional ceremonies are important to Native Americans.

Correct Answers, Part A _____

Correct Answers, Part B _____

Total Correct Answers _____

The ancient Egyptians built different kinds of monuments, including pyramids, sphinxes, and temples. The ruins of some of them are still standing.

The pyramids were tombs for the pharaohs, or kings. The Great Pyramid at Giza is the largest of them, covering about 12 acres of ground. The pyramids were built of huge sandstone blocks. The builders left spaces, or chambers, inside. The king was buried in one chamber, and a treasure chamber held things the king would need in the afterlife. These included food, gold, and furniture.

A sphinx is a statue with the body of a lion. The head might be that of a different animal or of a king. The Great Sphinx is also located at Giza. It is carved from the bedrock, which is sandstone. It is about 65 feet high, 13 feet wide, and 250 feet long. Experts think it was built before 2500 B.C. The head could be a likeness of King Khafre because it stands near his pyramid. A story appears on a stone slab between the paws. A prince fell asleep in the shade of the sphinx. Sand had covered and worn down the body of the sphinx. The sphinx told the prince that the prince would be king if he restored the statue. The prince restored it and became King Tutmose IV.

The temples of ancient Egypt were shrines to the gods. They were built of tall stone columns and giant blocks of stone. Later kings often enlarged a temple that another king had built. The temple of Karnak was built over a period of 1,300 years. The temple complex of about 200 acres is on the east bank of the Nile River. Amun, Mut, and Khonsu are the three main temples in the complex. The temple of Amun has a great hypostyle hall, a building with a roof supported by columns. It was built by Kings Seti I and Ramses II. The roof was once about 80 feet high. The inside walls are decorated with religious symbols, and the outside walls show battle scenes. Other temples and a sacred lake are at the complex. Another temple complex is nearby at Luxor. It was started about 1200 B.C. and built by several pharoahs. It is connected to the Karnak complex by a street about two miles long. Hundreds of sphinxes line both sides of the street.

Reading Time _____

Recalling Facts

1. The pyramids of ancient Egypt were
   - ❑ a. tombs for the pharaohs.
   - ❑ b. shrines to the gods.
   - ❑ c. great hypostyle halls.

2. The Great Pyramid is at
   - ❑ a. Karnak.
   - ❑ b. Luxor.
   - ❑ c. Giza.

3. A sphinx is a statue
   - ❑ a. of an Egyptian prince.
   - ❑ b. with the body of a lion and the head of a different animal or a king.
   - ❑ c. with the body of a human being and the head of a lion.

4. The prince who restored the Great Sphinx later became King
   - ❑ a. Seti I.
   - ❑ b. Ramses II.
   - ❑ c. Tutmose IV.

5. The temple complexes at Karnak and Luxor are connected by
   - ❑ a. the Nile River.
   - ❑ b. a street, lined with hundreds of sphinxes.
   - ❑ c. a sacred lake.

Understanding Ideas

6. From the passage, one can infer that sandstone
   - ❑ a. had to be transported to Egypt from distant lands.
   - ❑ b. is a natural resource of Egypt.
   - ❑ c. was not a good building material for the climate in Egypt.

7. An archaeologist would be most likely to find a pharaoh's treasures in a
   - ❑ a. pyramid.
   - ❑ b. temple.
   - ❑ c. sphinx.

8. It seems most likely that the pharaohs believed that
   - ❑ a. they would use objects from this life after they died.
   - ❑ b. they would have the body of a lion in the afterlife.
   - ❑ c. they would live in a sacred lake in the afterlife.

9. From facts given in the passage, one can infer that the Great Sphinx
   - ❑ a. was like a funny cartoon character for the ancient Egyptians.
   - ❑ b. was built to scare Egyptians.
   - ❑ c. was a symbol of power and greatness.

10. Which of the following sentences tells what the whole passage is about?
    - ❑ a. The pyramids were built of huge stone blocks.
    - ❑ b. The monuments of ancient Egypt are its pyramids, sphinxes, and temples.
    - ❑ c. A temple was started by one king and enlarged by others.

18   B   Who Built the Pyramids?

The Great Pyramid at Giza is about 480 feet high. It is made from more than 2 million stone blocks, and each block weighs about 2.5 tons. In the past, no one knew who built the pyramids. Some people thought that aliens did; others thought that a lost civilization did.

Recent evidence shows that the Egyptians themselves built the pyramids. Tomb paintings show the process. First, workers cut stones in a quarry near the pyramids. Then a team dragged a stone to the pyramid while other teams built a ramp. Next, the stone was pulled up the ramp. Finally, a team put the stone in place. Researcher Mark Lehner used these same techniques to move stone blocks. He proved that 20 men could drag a 2.5-ton block to the pyramid in less than 30 minutes. Four thousand people could have built the Great Pyramid in 25 years.

In the late 1980s, explorers found ruins of the city where the workers lived. They found many fish and cattle bones, enough to feed thousands of people for a century. They also found workers' tombs. X-rays of the bones show that these people labored hard. There was wear on their spines and joints, and some workers had broken bones that had healed. They probably broke the bones in accidents while building the pyramids.

1. **Recognizing Words in Context**

   Find the word *labored* in the passage. One definition below is closest to the meaning of that word. One definition has the opposite or nearly the opposite meaning. The remaining definition has a completely different meaning. Label the definitions C for *closest*, O for *opposite or nearly opposite*, and D for *different*.

   _____ a. collected

   _____ b. worked

   _____ c. rested

2. **Distinguishing Fact from Opinion**

   Two of the statements below present *facts*, which can be proved. The other statement is an *opinion*, which expresses someone's thoughts or beliefs. Label the statements F for *fact* and O for *opinion*.

   _____ a. The Great Pyramid at Giza is about 480 feet high.

   _____ b. Human beings could never have built the pyramids.

   _____ c. In the late 1980s, ruins of the city where the workers lived were found.

3. Keeping Events in Order

Number the statements below 1, 2, and 3 to show the order in which the events took place.

_____ a. The stone was put in place in the pyramid.

_____ b. A team dragged a stone to the pyramid.

_____ c. The stone was pulled up a ramp.

4. Making Correct Inferences

Two of the statements below are correct *inferences,* or reasonable guesses. They are based on information in the passage. The other statement is an incorrect, or faulty, inference. Label the statements C for *correct* inference and F for *faulty* inference.

_____ a. There have been different ideas about who built the pyramids.

_____ b. Many kinds of skilled workers were needed.

_____ c. Because they worked in teams, each worker did not have to work very hard.

5. Understanding Main Ideas

One of the statements below expresses the main idea of the passage. One statement is too general, or too broad. The other explains only part of the passage; it is too narrow. Label the statements M for *main idea,* B for *too broad,* and N for *too narrow.*

_____ a. Evidence found in ruins and tomb paintings show that ancient Egyptians built the pyramids.

_____ b. The Egyptians built huge monuments.

_____ c. X-rays of the bones of the pyramid workers show wear on the spines and joints.

Correct Answers, Part A _____

Correct Answers, Part B _____

Total Correct Answers _____

Since ancient times, people have watched birds soar and have dreamed of flying. These dreams sometimes became myths, stories, and art. In a Greek myth, a king trapped Daedalus and his son, Icarus, in a maze. Daedalus made wings of wax so that they could fly away, but Icarus flew too close to the sun. His wings melted, and he fell into the sea. A coin of ancient Babylonia showed the king flying on an eagle's back. The Inca claimed that one of their ancestors had wings and could fly.

Perhaps the first people to get off the ground were the Chinese. In about 1000 B.C., they made large kites that carried men to spy on enemy troops. In about 1100, in Turkey, a man made wings of pleated fabric. He jumped from a tower and fell to his death. Centuries later a man in France built wings that flapped, using a spring. The spring broke and cost him his life. In the fifteenth century, artist Leonardo da Vinci drew flying machines.

In 1783, in France, the Montgolfier brothers built a hot air balloon. First they sent up a duck, a rooster, and a sheep; then they went up themselves for a four-minute flight. The first woman to lose her life while flying was Marie Blanchard. She was watching fireworks from her balloon. The balloon used hydrogen gas, which caught fire.

Samuel Pierpont Langley in 1896 made a steam-powered aircraft that flew several times. In 1892 Orville and Wilbur Wright opened a bicycle shop in Ohio. There the brothers built a flying machine powered by an engine. In 1903 they went to Kitty Hawk, North Carolina, to fly their airplane. The Wright Flyer was the first craft heavier than air to fly with a pilot. (Balloons used heat or gas to make them lighter than air.) The flight of 121 feet took just 12 seconds. The Wright brothers improved their plane and made longer and longer flights. They went on to sell planes to France, Britain, and the United States. In the years that followed, people and mail traveled by plane.

While the Wrights built planes, young Robert Goddard dreamed of rockets. Goddard grew up to be a scientist. He made many rockets that did not fly, but in 1926 he made one that did. It was the first rocket to fly on liquid fuel. In 1969 a rocket would carry people to the moon.

Reading Time _____

Recalling Facts

1. In a Greek myth, Daedalus made
   _____ so he and his son could
   escape from a maze.
   - ❏ a. a large kite
   - ❏ b. a rocket
   - ❏ c. wings of wax

2. It is believed that the first people to
   get off the ground were the
   - ❏ a. Chinese.
   - ❏ b. British.
   - ❏ c. French.

3. Leonardo da Vinci was
   - ❏ a. a rocket scientist.
   - ❏ b. an artist who drew flying
     machines.
   - ❏ c. the first man to fly a plane.

4. The inventors of the hot air balloon
   were
   - ❏ a. the Montgolfier brothers.
   - ❏ b. the Wright brothers.
   - ❏ c. Marie Blanchard and Jules
     Verne.

5. Robert Goddard invented
   - ❏ a. the first airplane.
   - ❏ b. the first rocket to fly on liquid
     fuel.
   - ❏ c. hydrogen.

Understanding Ideas

6. From the passage, one can infer that
   early people dreamed of flying
   because they wanted to
   - ❏ a. explore the clouds.
   - ❏ b. visit other planets.
   - ❏ c. soar like the birds.

7. From the passage, one can infer that
   the dream of flying
   - ❏ a. was based on the Greek myth of
     Daedalus and the wax wings.
   - ❏ b. inspired many ideas and
     inventions through the ages.
   - ❏ c. was of interest only to famous
     artists and writers.

8. The saying or proverb that best
   summarizes the passage is
   - ❏ a. It's as easy as falling off a log.
   - ❏ b. Where there is a will, there is a
     way.
   - ❏ c. Leave well enough alone.

9. An early flying machine that did *not*
   use an engine was
   - ❏ a. a hot air balloon.
   - ❏ b. an airplane.
   - ❏ c. a rocket.

10. From the passage, one can infer that
    human attempts to fly
    - ❏ a. have not been successful.
    - ❏ b. began after Leonardo da Vinci
      drew flying machines.
    - ❏ c. cost many lives through the
      ages.

Amelia Earhart

Amelia Earhart was born in Kansas in 1898. As a young girl, she loved to climb trees. She also kept a scrapbook about women who held jobs usually done by men.

At age 22, Earhart rode in an airplane. Once in the air, she knew she wanted to fly. She took flying lessons and saved money to buy a used plane. She set a new woman's record by flying to an altitude of 14,000 feet. In 1932 she became the first woman to make a solo flight across the Atlantic Ocean. She flew through strong, icy winds. She planned to land in Paris, but engine problems forced her to land in Ireland. The United States Congress awarded her the Distinguished Flying Cross.

Earhart wanted to be the first woman to fly around the world. She and her navigator left Miami, Florida, in 1937. By the time they reached New Guinea, they had flown more than 22,000 miles. Their next stop was Howland Island, more than 2,000 miles away. Earhart took everything unneeded out of the plane to carry more fuel. Rain made it impossible to use the sky to navigate. In her final radio message, Earhart said that she was low on fuel. She could not see the island. Rescuers searched for weeks, but Earhart's plane was never found.

1. **Recognizing Words in Context**

   Find the word *solo* in the passage. One definition below is closest to the meaning of that word. One definition has the opposite or nearly the opposite meaning. The remaining definition has a completely different meaning. Label the definitions C for *closest*, O for *opposite or nearly opposite*, and D for *different*.

   _____ a. at the end

   _____ b. with others

   _____ c. by oneself

2. **Distinguishing Fact from Opinion**

   Two of the statements below present *facts*, which can be proved. The other statement is an *opinion*, which expresses someone's thoughts or beliefs. Label the statements F for *fact* and O for *opinion*.

   _____ a. At age 22, Earhart rode in a plane and knew she wanted to fly.

   _____ b. The U.S. Congress awarded Earhart the Distinguished Flying Cross.

   _____ c. Earhart was foolish to try to fly around the world.

3. Keeping Events in Order

Number the statements below 1, 2, and 3 to show the order in which the events took place.

_____ a. Rain made it impossible to use the sky to navigate.

_____ b. Earhart and her navigator left New Guinea to fly to Howland Island.

_____ c. In a message, Earhart said that she was low on fuel and couldn't see the island.

4. Making Correct Inferences

Two of the statements below are correct *inferences*, or reasonable guesses. They are based on information in the passage. The other statement is an incorrect, or faulty, inference. Label the statements C for *correct* inference and F for *faulty* inference.

_____ a. Amelia Earhart was a brave and daring woman.

_____ b. Earhart was an accomplished and famous woman pilot.

_____ c. Earhart was the first woman to pilot a plane.

5. Understanding Main Ideas

One of the statements below expresses the main idea of the passage. One statement is too general, or too broad. The other explains only part of the passage; it is too narrow. Label the statements M for *main idea*, B for *too broad*, and N for *too narrow*.

_____ a. Amelia Earhart was an exceptional pilot.

_____ b. There have been many famous pilots in U.S. history.

_____ c. In 1932 Earhart made a solo flight across the Atlantic.

Correct Answers, Part A _____

Correct Answers, Part B _____

Total Correct Answers _____

The History of the American Public Library System

The first libraries in the New World were private ones. People owned them for their own personal use. In the 1700s some colonies began subscription libraries. Members paid dues that were used to buy books. Benjamin Franklin started one of the first of these. In the West there were "coonskin" libraries. People could pay their dues with raccoon pelts. In the 1800s, more kinds of libraries came into existence. Mercantile libraries were run by and for merchants. People learning a trade used apprentice libraries.

In 1800 the United States Congress started its own library. It was destroyed during the War of 1812 when the British burned Washington. Congress then bought Thomas Jefferson's books to restart the library. Today the Library of Congress is the world's largest library.

A public library belongs to a community. It is free for the people who live there. One of the first public libraries in the United States began in 1771. It started as a subscription library. Richard Smith of Salisbury, Connecticut, collected funds to buy books. Books could be checked out and returned on a few days of the year. If a book showed signs of damage, the user was fined. One kind of damage was wax on the books. This came from the candles used for light to read by. Later more books were purchased with town money. Then all of the townspeople could use the library.

Massachusetts was home to another early public library. Part of the town of Wrentham broke off from the rest of the town. The new town had a church but no bell. The people thought of an idea for how to get a bell. They named the new town Franklin, after Benjamin Franklin. They asked Franklin to give them a bell. Franklin, saying "sense being preferable to sound," gave them some books instead to start a library with.

In the late 1800s public libraries spread across the land. This was due in part to philanthropy. Those who could afford to gave funds to start libraries for the good of all. One wealthy contributor was Andrew Carnegie. He grew up poor but made a fortune in the steel business. He thought that a library was one of the best things a community could give its people. He helped build more than 2,000 public libraries.

Today most public libraries are part of a library system. The libraries that make up the system share books and services.

Reading Time _____

Recalling Facts

1. The first libraries in the New World were
   - ❑ a. public libraries.
   - ❑ b. run by Congress.
   - ❑ c. private libraries.

2. A library whose members pay dues that are used to buy books is a
   - ❑ a. subscription library.
   - ❑ b. apprentice library.
   - ❑ c. merchant library.

3. After the Library of Congress was burned, Congress bought books from _____ to restart the library.
   - ❑ a. Richard Smith
   - ❑ b. Thomas Jefferson
   - ❑ c. Benjamin Franklin

4. A public library belongs to
   - ❑ a. a community.
   - ❑ b. an individual.
   - ❑ c. a group of business people.

5. Andrew Carnegie
   - ❑ a. gave books instead of a church bell to a town in Massachusetts.
   - ❑ b. started a "coonskin" library in the West.
   - ❑ c. thought a library was one of the best things a community could give its people.

Understanding Ideas

6. From the passage, one can infer that Americans
   - ❑ a. have looked for ways to fund and support libraries since early times.
   - ❑ b. prefer to own the books they read.
   - ❑ c. rarely use public libraries.

7. When Benjamin Franklin said, "sense being preferable to sound," he probably meant that
   - ❑ a. sight is a more useful sense than hearing.
   - ❑ b. one should be sound in both mind and body.
   - ❑ c. knowledge gained from reading a book is worth more than hearing a bell.

8. Benjamin Franklin and Thomas Jefferson
   - ❑ a. were interested in starting a mercantile library.
   - ❑ b. valued books.
   - ❑ c. started a library together.

9. From the passage, one can infer that today's public libraries
   - ❑ a. started out as private libraries.
   - ❑ b. became established in a variety of ways.
   - ❑ c. were started by the Library of Congress.

10. From the passage, one can infer that a public library's main purpose is to
    - ❑ a. give many people access to books and other sources of information.
    - ❑ b. share books and services with other libraries in a system.
    - ❑ c. make money for the community.

When doing research on a topic, you might find the Internet a good source of information. A person looking for social studies data can follow these three steps.

Step 1: Use a "Web directory" or a "search engine." Web directories organize the World Wide Web by topics and subtopics. Go to a Web directory to find general facts on a broad topic. A search engine is organized differently. It is a huge index of Web data. A person can use a search engine by entering keywords such as *Civil War.* If the keywords return hundreds of sites, the user should then narrow the search. Search engines have different methods to make the search more specific. There are also search engines just for history, maps, and biographies.

Step 2: Make sure each source is reliable. Check out who wrote the material. The official White House site has more authority than a tourist company's home page. Online encyclopedias and museums are good sources. Finding more than one source with the same data is one way to verify the facts.

Step 3: Choose from among sources to get a balanced view. To learn about famous people, read what they wrote about themselves. Then read what others wrote about them. For example, to learn more about a war, read what people on both sides have written.

1. **Recognizing Words in Context**

Find the word *reliable* in the passage. One definition below is closest to the meaning of that word. One definition has the opposite or nearly the opposite meaning. The remaining definition has a completely different meaning. Label the definitions C for *closest,* O for *opposite or nearly opposite,* and D for *different.*

_____ a. dependable

_____ b. enjoyable

_____ c. untrustworthy

2. **Distinguishing Fact from Opinion**

Two of the statements below present *facts,* which can be proved. The other statement is an *opinion,* which expresses someone's thoughts or beliefs. Label the statements F for *fact* and O for *opinion.*

_____ a. A search engine is a huge index of Web information.

_____ b. There are search engines for history, maps, and biographies.

_____ c. It is easier to find topics for social studies in books than on the Internet.

3. **Keeping Events in Order**
Number the statements below 1, 2, and 3 to show the order in which the events took place.

_____ a. Look through the list of Web sites and determine which ones are reliable.

_____ b. Choose among the reliable sources and read to get a balanced view.

_____ c. Use a Web directory or a search engine to find information on a topic.

4. **Making Correct Inferences**
Two of the statements below are correct *inferences,* or reasonable guesses. They are based on information in the passage. The other statement is an incorrect, or faulty, inference. Label the statements C for *correct* inference and F for *faulty* inference.

_____ a. Not all information on the Internet is reliable.

_____ b. Web directories and search engines are useful research tools.

_____ c. The Internet is always a better source of information than books or magazines.

5. **Understanding Main Ideas**
One of the statements below expresses the main idea of the passage. One statement is too general, or too broad. The other explains only part of the passage; it is too narrow. Label the statements M for *main idea*, B for *too broad*, and N for *too narrow*.

_____ a. The Internet was an important invention.

_____ b. Online encyclopedias are sources for social studies topics.

_____ c. Following three main steps can help you do social studies research on the Internet.

Correct Answers, Part A _____

Correct Answers, Part B _____

Total Correct Answers _____

The Maya were a group that was native to Mexico and parts of Central America. Before Columbus arrived in the New World, the Maya built great cities. The ruins of their temples and pyramids are still standing today.

The Classic Period of Mayan civilization lasted from about A.D. 300 to 900. A king ruled each group. When the king died, his son became king. Before a new king could take the throne, he had to capture an enemy. The captive was killed and offered as a blood sacrifice when the new king took power.

The king, his family, priests, scholars, and architects were the noble elite. Artists and craftsmen made up a middle class. Workers and slaves made up the lower classes. Warriors were a separate class. That class also included farmers in times of war. Mayan people were part of the social class into which they were born.

Farming was the primary basis of Mayan life. Farmers grew beans, squash, maize (corn), and cotton. They also hunted and fished. Mayan craftsmen wove beautiful cloth. They also made pottery. They used gold, silver, and jade ornaments. They cut routes through the jungle so that they could trade these goods with distant peoples.

The Mayan religion included many gods, such as a creator god, a sky god, and a god of rain. Priests were very important. They were the only ones who were thought to understand the wishes of the gods.

The Maya were brilliant mathematicians and scientists. They were the first people to use place value and the zero. They used geometry in their buildings. Their accurate calendars were based on their observations of the Sun and the Moon.

Mayan writing was partially made up of picture symbols called hieroglyphs. The Maya wrote about weather, hunting, religion, and history. They carved some of their writings on stone buildings and monuments. They used paints to write "books," which were made from the soft bark of fig trees. Only four of these books, or codices, are known to exist today.

The Maya abandoned their cities in the tenth century. Some scientists believe that war, possibly a peasant revolt, may have caused them to leave. Burn marks on buildings and war images on pots and monuments show that war probably took place. The ruins also suggest that many people lived in the cities. During a drought, there may not have been enough water or food for a large population.

Reading Time _____

Recalling Facts

1. The Maya lived in Mexico and
   - ❑ a. parts of Peru.
   - ❑ b. parts of Central America.
   - ❑ c. Arizona.

2. Mayan artists and craftsmen belonged to the
   - ❑ a. noble elite.
   - ❑ b. middle class.
   - ❑ c. warrior class.

3. According to the article, the Maya were the first people to
   - ❑ a. use fire.
   - ❑ b. farm.
   - ❑ c. use a zero.

4. The symbols that the Maya used for words are called
   - ❑ a. codices.
   - ❑ b. ruins.
   - ❑ c. hieroglyphs.

5. In the tenth century, the Maya
   - ❑ a. abandoned their cities.
   - ❑ b. held a great celebration.
   - ❑ c. migrated to the New World.

Understanding Ideas

6. After reading the information in the passage, one can conclude that the Maya
   - ❑ a. lived a very simple life.
   - ❑ b. were an intelligent and creative people.
   - ❑ c. did not have contact with other peoples.

7. From the passage, it seems most likely that in a Mayan tribe
   - ❑ a. a craftsman could easily join the noble elite.
   - ❑ b. all people were equal.
   - ❑ c. it was difficult to move from one class to another.

8. Of the following, the person most likely to tell other Maya what to do was
   - ❑ a. a craftsman.
   - ❑ b. a priest.
   - ❑ c. a warrior.

9. One can conclude that Mayan society
   - ❑ a. was highly organized.
   - ❑ b. was made up mainly of hunters and farmers.
   - ❑ c. had little use for mathematics.

10. The Maya probably abandoned their cities because of
    - ❑ a. their desire for a simpler life in the country.
    - ❑ b. a major change in climate.
    - ❑ c. a combination of war, drought, and overpopulation.

21   B   The Mayan Calendars

The Maya were one of the earliest peoples to use calendars. They based the calendars on observations of the heavens and on mathematical knowledge.

The Mayans used three calendars. One, the Long Count, kept track of days, starting from a zero date in 3114 B.C. A *kin* was one day. A total of 20 kin made up a *uinal,* or month. Eighteen uinal made up a *tun,* or year.

The Tzolkin, or divine calendar, had two kinds of weeks. One had 13 numbered days, and the second had 20 days that had names. The cycles of numbered weeks and named weeks ran concurrently, or at the same time. The Maya wrote dates as a combination of the concurrent numbered day and the named day. At the beginning of a year, the priests held a special ceremony, during which they pointed out the days to plant and the days of religious ceremonies.

The third Mayan calendar, the Haab, had 365 days and was based on the position of the Sun over a year. There was the *tun* (18 months made up of 20 days each). At the end were five extra days, called *Uayeb.* These days were unlucky, and Mayans spent them in prayer or mourning.

The Tzolkin and the Haab ran at the same time: Dates were written showing the position of both on each calendar.

1. Recognizing Words in Context

Find the word *concurrently* in the passage. One definition below is closest to the meaning of that word. One definition has the opposite or nearly the opposite meaning. The remaining definition has a completely different meaning. Label the definitions C for *closest,* O for *opposite or nearly opposite,* and D for *different.*

_____ a. at different times

_____ b. at the same time

_____ c. twice a week

2. Distinguishing Fact from Opinion

Two of the statements below present *facts,* which can be proved. The other statement is an *opinion,* which expresses someone's thoughts or beliefs. Label the statements F for *fact* and O for *opinion.*

_____ a. In the Long Count, a kin is one day.

_____ b. The Mayan calendars were too complicated.

_____ c. The Tzolkin and the Haab ran at the same time.

3. Keeping Events in Order

Number the statements below 1, 2, and 3 to show the order in which the events took place.

_____ a. The people followed the calendar.

_____ b. At the end of 260 days, the next Tzolkin (religious) year began.

_____ c. The priests pointed out the correct dates on which to plant and the dates of religious ceremonies.

4. Making Correct Inferences

Two of the statements below are correct *inferences,* or reasonable guesses. They are based on information in the passage. The other statement is an incorrect, or faulty, inference. Label the statements C for *correct* inference and F for *faulty* inference.

_____ a. The Maya knew a great deal about the movements of the planets.

_____ b. If the Mayan calendars were accurate, the one people use today is not so good.

_____ c. Each of the Mayan calendars had a special purpose.

5. Understanding Main Ideas

One of the statements below expresses the main idea of the passage. One statement is too general, or too broad. The other explains only part of the passage; it is too narrow. Label the statements M for *main idea,* B for *too broad,* and N for *too narrow.*

_____ a. The Tzolkin, or divine calendar, had two kinds of weeks.

_____ b. The Maya used three kinds of calendars that ran at the same time.

_____ c. Calendars are used by people around the world.

Correct Answers, Part A _____

Correct Answers, Part B _____

Total Correct Answers _____

In 1792 work began on building a home for the United States' president. It would be located in the nation's new capital city—Washington, D.C. Architect James Hoban entered his design for the new building in a contest and won. At the time, George Washington was in office. He supervised the work. He wanted it to be as grand as a palace but comfortable to live in. Hoban's plan was in the style of a British country house. The walls were built of gray sandstone. When Washington left office, the house had only walls and a roof frame. President John Adams moved into the house in 1801.

During the War of 1812, the president's house was destroyed. In August of 1814, Britain and the United States were still at war. The British landed their forces about 50 miles from the city. The American troops tried to stop them in Maryland but failed. Two miles from Washington, the troops again made a stand. President James Madison was with them, watching the battle. Finally, the British forced the Americans to retreat to the city.

The first lady, Dolley Madison, was waiting at home. She got word that the British were on their way. She had a portrait of George Washington removed from its frame and took it with her when she fled. When British troops entered the house, they found the dining room set for guests. Earlier, a feast had been cooked for the American troops to eat after they won the battle. First the British ate dinner; then they set fire to the house. The sandstone walls and some brickwork were all that remained after the fire.

Over the next three years, Hoban rebuilt the house, using the original walls. At this time, the sandstone walls were painted white, and the house was nicknamed the "White House." Later, Theodore Roosevelt made this name official. He also had the West Wing built. The president's office was moved there.

By 1948 the White House was an old building. Some thought it might collapse. During Harry S. Truman's term, the inside walls were torn out. All the rooms were rebuilt. When John F. Kennedy was president, First Lady Jacqueline Kennedy redecorated the White House. Today there is still a square of unpainted wall on a balcony. One can see on it the marks from the fire. The portrait of Washington that Dolley Madison saved hangs in the East Room.

Reading Time _____

Recalling Facts

1. The architect _____ built the president's home.
   - ❑ a. James Madison
   - ❑ b. James Hoban
   - ❑ c. John Adams

2. The walls of the president's home were built of
   - ❑ a. gray sandstone.
   - ❑ b. white limestone.
   - ❑ c. red brick.

3. The British burned the president's home during the
   - ❑ a. Civil War.
   - ❑ b. Revolutionary War.
   - ❑ c. War of 1812.

4. When Dolley Madison fled from the British troops, she took with her a portrait of
   - ❑ a. George Washington.
   - ❑ b. James Madison.
   - ❑ c. Theodore Roosevelt.

5. The nickname "White House" was made official by President
   - ❑ a. Harry S. Truman.
   - ❑ b. Theodore Roosevelt.
   - ❑ c. John F. Kennedy.

Understanding Ideas

6. From the passage, one can conclude that George Washington
   - ❑ a. was the first president to live in the White House.
   - ❑ b. never lived in the White House.
   - ❑ c. was disappointed with the work of James Hoban.

7. From the passage, one can infer that the White House
   - ❑ a. will probably have some changes in the future.
   - ❑ b. has been unchanged since it was rebuilt after the War of 1812.
   - ❑ c. is the same size today as it was when it was first built.

8. From the passage, one can infer that
   - ❑ a. it is not important where the president lives.
   - ❑ b. the White House will be rebuilt someday at another location outside Washington, D.C.
   - ❑ c. keeping the original outside walls is an important symbol of endurance.

9. From the passage, one can conclude that Dolley Madison
   - ❑ a. had expected the United States to defeat the British.
   - ❑ b. had little confidence in the American army.
   - ❑ c. did not like to entertain guests.

10. Which of the following sentences tells what the whole passage is about?
    - ❑ a. The White House got its name from its white walls.
    - ❑ b. The White House has an interesting history.
    - ❑ c. Many presidents have lived in the White House.

White House Tour

On a White House tour, visitors enter through the East Wing. This wing houses the First Lady's office and the president's theater. Visitors then walk between a long series of columns. Finally, they enter the president's residence to view its many rooms.

The East Room is where dances, concerts, weddings, and funerals are held. Seven presidents who died in office have lain in state in this room.

The Green Room, Blue Room, and Red Room are named only for their colors. The Green Room has been a guest room, a dining room, and a card room. The Blue Room is oval in shape. There one can see furniture gilded, or painted gold. A portrait of First Lady Dolley Madison hangs in the Red Room. She gave card parties and served ice cream there.

In the Map Room, visitors see many maps, including rare maps and world maps. This room was used during World War II for studying maps of the war campaigns.

The West Wing is where the president works. As its name indicates, the Cabinet Room is where the president meets with members of the Cabinet. In the Oval Office, he works at his desk, meets with his staff, and talks with leaders from other countries. In more recent times, presidents have also used this room when talking to the American people on TV or radio.

1. **Recognizing Words in Context**

   Find the word *indicates* in the passage. One definition below is closest to the meaning of that word. One definition has the opposite or nearly the opposite meaning. The remaining definition has a completely different meaning. Label the definitions C for *closest*, O for *opposite or nearly opposite*, and D for *different*.

   _____ a. hides

   _____ b. reveals

   _____ c. worries

2. **Distinguishing Fact from Opinion**

   Two of the statements below present *facts*, which can be proved. The other statement is an *opinion*, which expresses someone's thoughts or beliefs. Label the statements F for *fact* and O for *opinion*.

   _____ a. In the Red Room is a portrait of Dolley Madison.

   _____ b. The West Wing is where the president works.

   _____ c. The White House is the most beautiful building in Washington.

3. Keeping Events in Order

Number the statements below 1, 2, and 3 to show the order in which the events took place.

_____ a. Visitors enter the residence.

_____ b. Visitors walk between a long series of columns.

_____ c. Visitors enter through the East Wing.

4. Making Correct Inferences

Two of the statements below are correct *inferences*, or reasonable guesses. They are based on information in the passage. The other statement is an incorrect, or faulty, inference. Label the statements C for *correct* inference and F for *faulty* inference.

_____ a. The West Wing is the work center of the White House.

_____ b. The rooms in the White House have been used at different times for different purposes.

_____ c. Every room in the White House is named for a different color.

5. Understanding Main Ideas

One of the statements below expresses the main idea of the passage. One statement is too general, or too broad. The other explains only part of the passage; it is too narrow. Label the statements M for *main idea*, B for *too broad*, and N for *too narrow*.

_____ a. On a White House tour, one can see many rooms in the president's residence.

_____ b. Many people, including world leaders, visit the White House.

_____ c. The Map Room was used during World War II to view maps of the war.

Correct Answers, Part A _____

Correct Answers, Part B _____

Total Correct Answers _____

National Women's History Month

Today women in the United States have many rights. They have the right to vote and to get an education. They have the right to expect a fair wage for their work. They may take part in school sports, serve in the armed forces, and hold political offices. American women have these rights today because other women fought to win them. Their hard work and sacrifices changed laws. These women and their stories are part of an important field of study called women's history.

Before 1978 most schools did not teach women's history. A group in California set out to change that. These women organized Women's History Week. They chose to celebrate it the week of March 8, which is International Women's Day. This date would ensure that the week would focus on women from many cultures. Many women became involved. They went to schools to give talks, and they held essay contests and history parades. The following March, more groups held more events.

In 1980 the National Women's History Project was founded. One of its main goals was to tell about the March event. It also put together materials to help schools teach women's history. Since the first Women's History Week, the event has grown. Events to celebrate it take place through the whole month of March. National Women's History Month is now a huge event.

Each year the event has a theme. One theme was "Women Sustaining the American Spirit." The goal was to tell the stories of women who helped shape the spirit of the country. Gerda Lerner is one of these women. Lerner grew up in Europe. As a teen, she worked against the Nazis and was put in prison. Later the Nazis forced her to leave her country. She came to the United States, where she worked for civil rights and better schools in New York.

Alice Coachman is another woman of note. In 1948 she became the first African American woman to win an Olympic gold medal in track and field. She also broke the Olympic record for the high jump. Coachman grew up in the South. At the time, segregation was legal. African Americans could not use the same facilities as others. Because she had no place to train, Coachman ran barefoot on dirt roads. She made her own jumps from strings and sticks. She proved that a woman could be a top athlete.

Reading Time _____

Recalling Facts

1. Woman's History Month is
   - ❑ a. March.
   - ❑ b. April.
   - ❑ c. May.

2. Women's History Week coincides with the celebration of International Women's Day so that it would
   - ❑ a. be celebrated in other countries.
   - ❑ b. focus on international issues and politics.
   - ❑ c. focus on women from many cultures.

3. One main goal of the National Women's History Project is to
   - ❑ a. make Women's History Month a yearlong event.
   - ❑ b. provide information about the March event.
   - ❑ c. hold parades.

4. As a teen, Gerda Lerner
   - ❑ a. worked against the Nazis.
   - ❑ b. founded National Women's History Month.
   - ❑ c. started International Women's Day.

5. Alice Coachman
   - ❑ a. started the National Women's History Project.
   - ❑ b. won an Olympic gold medal.
   - ❑ c. worked for better schools in New York City.

Understanding Ideas

6. One can conclude that National Women's History Month
   - ❑ a. is really a week long.
   - ❑ b. began in Europe.
   - ❑ c. has become very popular.

7. One can conclude that the National Women's History Project
   - ❑ a. involved the efforts of many.
   - ❑ b. honored history teachers.
   - ❑ c. mostly helped to raise money for poor women.

8. Which of the following sentences tells what the passage is about?
   - ❑ a. National Women's History Month encourages us to read about women's history.
   - ❑ b. National Women's History Month promotes education about women's struggles to win civil rights.
   - ❑ c. National Women's History Month is an important part of International Women's Day.

9. From the passage, one can conclude that women's history is
   - ❑ a. taught more in schools now than before 1978.
   - ❑ b. more important than world history.
   - ❑ c. about women who came to the United States from abroad.

10. The article suggests that Coachman
    - ❑ a. won a gold medal even though she was not able to practice.
    - ❑ b. found ways to solve problems.
    - ❑ c. was not affected by discrimination during the 1940s.

Dolores Huerta: Labor Leader

Dolores Huerta was born in 1930 in New Mexico. After graduating from college, she became a teacher. The school where she taught was in a farming district. The farmworkers were poor. They lived and worked under terrible conditions.

Huerta wanted to do something to help the farmworkers. She began by helping them to register to vote. She also urged them to work for change. In a few years' time, she and another Hispanic leader, Cesar Chavez, helped farmworkers to form a group. This group, the United Farm Workers Union (UFW), worked for change. Members used nonviolent protest. For example, grape growers did not want to accept the union. Huerta helped to lead a boycott of grapes. She asked people not to buy grapes until the growers would work with the UFW. It took five years, but the boycott worked. The grape growers signed the agreement. This made the workers' lives better.

Huerta went on to represent the UFW in Washington, D.C. She worked to get the Agricultural Labor Relations Act passed. This act gave farmworkers the right to organize. They can now bargain as a group for better living and working conditions. For more than 30 years, Huerta has worked for the union. She is an example of how women can cause change that makes people's lives better.

1. **Recognizing Words in Context**

   Find the word *nonviolent* in the passage. One definition below is closest to the meaning of that word. One definition has the opposite or nearly the opposite meaning. The remaining definition has a completely different meaning. Label the definitions C for *closest*, O for *opposite or nearly opposite*, and D for *different*.

   _____ a. with force

   _____ b. peaceful

   _____ c. grateful

2. **Distinguishing Fact from Opinion**

   Two of the statements below present *facts*, which can be proved. The other statement is an *opinion*, which expresses someone's thoughts or beliefs. Label the statements F for *fact* and O for *opinion*.

   _____ a. Huerta was born in 1930 in the state of New Mexico.

   _____ b. Huerta worked as a teacher in a poor farming district.

   _____ c. Huerta's efforts to help farmworkers were not as successful as those of Cesar Chavez.

3. Keeping Events in Order

Number the statements below 1, 2, and 3 to show the order in which the events took place.

_____ a. Huerta helped workers to register to vote.

_____ b. Huerta led a boycott of grapes.

_____ c. Huerta worked to get the Agricultural Labor Relations Act passed.

4. Making Correct Inferences

Two of the statements below are correct *inferences,* or reasonable guesses. They are based on information in the passage. The other statement is an incorrect, or faulty, inference. Label the statements C for *correct* inference and F for *faulty* inference.

_____ a. Huerta believes that people can bring about change by working together.

_____ b. Even after the boycott ended, Huerta did not believe anyone should eat grapes.

_____ c. Huerta has demonstrated leadership skills.

5. Understanding Main Ideas

One of the statements below expresses the main idea of the passage. One statement is too general, or too broad. The other explains only part of the passage; it is too narrow. Label the statements M for *main idea,* B for *too broad,* and N for *too narrow.*

_____ a. Dolores Huerta helped lead farmworkers to form a union, which made their lives better.

_____ b. Dolores Huerta taught school in a farming district.

_____ c. Several important acts helped the plight of the farmworker.

Correct Answers, Part A _____

Correct Answers, Part B _____

Total Correct Answers _____

The United States has a special system of federal government. The states and the national government share power. The U.S. Constitution tells how power is shared. It provides the framework for organizing the government.

The national government has three branches. The first is the legislative branch, or Congress. Its members represent the states. The job of Congress is to set national laws. The second branch is the executive branch. This includes the president and his cabinet. The job of this branch is to enforce the national laws. The third branch is the judicial branch. This includes the U.S. Supreme Court and the lower federal courts. The job of the courts is to interpret the law by judging cases that come before them. The Supreme Court has the power to overrule decisions of state courts in cases concerning the Constitution. The national government is run from the nation's capital in Washington, D.C. The national government can print money and declare war. It controls relations and trade with other nations and trade between the states.

State governments are run from the capital of each state. The chief executive of a state is the governor. A state legislature passes laws that define criminal behavior. States also create local governments and administer elections. Each state controls the trade in that state. Each state sees to the public health, safety, and education of its people.

Some powers are shared by both levels of government. Both can make laws. Both can collect taxes. The national government uses tax money to run the armed forces and to build roads. It also manages many other programs. The states use tax money to pay for state roads and parks. They also use it to pay for police, public schools, and colleges.

How the powers of government are shared has developed over time. Before the Civil War, for example, slavery and other issues caused deep divisions between people in the North and those in the South. The Civil War resulted when Southern states decided to break away from the Union. They wanted to form their own government. President Abraham Lincoln and Congress said that states did not have that power. The North won the war. The South remained in the Union. After the war, the Constitution was changed. Two amendments were made. The thirteenth outlaws slavery. The fourteenth protects the rights of all citizens.

Reading Time _____

Recalling Facts

1. In the United States federal government, power is shared
   - ❑ a. among the states.
   - ❑ b. by Congress and the Supreme Court.
   - ❑ c. by the states and the national government.

2. The job of Congress is to
   - ❑ a. set national laws.
   - ❑ b. make sure that the laws are obeyed.
   - ❑ c. make sure that the laws are fair.

3. The national government has the power to
   - ❑ a. print money and declare war.
   - ❑ b. control trade within a state.
   - ❑ c. see to the public safety of a state.

4. The power to collect taxes is
   - ❑ a. that of the national government only.
   - ❑ b. shared by the national and state governments.
   - ❑ c. that of the state governments only.

5. The national government uses its tax money to
   - ❑ a. build state colleges.
   - ❑ b. run the armed forces and build roads.
   - ❑ c. build state parks.

Understanding Ideas

6. Which of the following sentences tells what the whole passage is about?
   - ❑ a. The Constitution was changed after the Civil War.
   - ❑ b. The national government has three branches.
   - ❑ c. State and national power is shared in the U.S. federal system of government.

7. Which of the following laws does a state most likely have the power to pass?
   - ❑ a. Women can no longer vote.
   - ❑ b. The state will print its own money.
   - ❑ c. State parks will charge an admission fee.

8. Of the following, the tax a person in Ohio does *not* have to pay is
   - ❑ a. federal income tax.
   - ❑ b. Ohio income tax.
   - ❑ c. Michigan income tax.

9. If a state court makes a law that goes against the U.S. Constitution, the law
   - ❑ a. applies only to that state.
   - ❑ b. can be overturned by the Supreme Court.
   - ❑ c. will be adopted by all other states.

10. From the passage, one can infer that state laws are made in
    - ❑ a. the state capital.
    - ❑ b. Washington, D.C.
    - ❑ c. the Supreme Court.

Schools: A Part of Local Government

Each state has the primary authority for its public schools, but local government controls most school matters. Each state is divided into school districts. A district is a branch of local government. States establish departments of education, set requirements for teacher licenses, and regulate district finances. A school board oversees each school district. The voters of the district elect the members to the board. The board makes decisions about the schools in its district. The board decides the hours that school will be held. It hires and pays the teachers. It builds new schools as needed.

The money to run the schools comes from a variety of sources and varies from state to state. In most states, funds come from federal, state, and local taxes. Almost half of the funds to run most public schools comes from local government. Much of this money comes from property taxes. For this reason, the amount of money that individual school districts have varies widely. The local school board decides how the money is spent. For this reason, public schools are not all the same. If a school board decides that new schools are needed, it may hold an election, asking people to vote to raise taxes. If the voters agree, the board can use the tax increase to build new schools.

1. **Recognizing Words in Context**

   Find the word *variety* in the passage. One definition below is closest to the meaning of that word. One definition has the opposite or nearly the opposite meaning. The remaining definition has a completely different meaning. Label the definitions C for *closest*, O for *opposite or nearly opposite*, and D for *different*.

   _____ a. assortment

   _____ b. matching set

   _____ c. sponsor

2. **Distinguishing Fact from Opinion**

   Two of the statements below present *facts*, which can be proved. The other statement is an *opinion*, which expresses someone's thoughts or beliefs. Label the statements F for *fact* and O for *opinion*.

   _____ a. Sports programs are more important than computer labs.

   _____ b. The states are the main authority for the public schools.

   _____ c. Each school district is run by a school board.

3. Keeping Events in Order

Number the statements below 1, 2, and 3 to show the order in which the events took place.

_____ a. A school board decides whether money is needed for new buildings.

_____ b. If the voters agree to raise taxes, the board may build the new schools.

_____ c. An election is held.

4. Making Correct Inferences

Two of the statements below are correct *inferences,* or reasonable guesses. They are based on information in the passage. The other statement is an incorrect, or faulty, inference. Label the statements C for *correct* inference and F for *faulty* inference.

_____ a. A fifth-grader in one district may have a different social studies book from that of a fifth-grader in another district.

_____ b. Property taxes are an important source of public school funds.

_____ c. The states provide most of the money for the public schools.

5. Understanding Main Ideas

One of the statements below expresses the main idea of the passage. One statement is too general, or too broad. The other explains only part of the passage; it is too narrow. Label the statements M for *main idea,* B for *too broad,* and N for *too narrow.*

_____ a. Public schools are a part of local government.

_____ b. Every state has public schools.

_____ c. Almost half of the funds to run most public schools comes from local government.

Correct Answers, Part A _____

Correct Answers, Part B _____

Total Correct Answers _____

Grant's Tomb: A National Monument

Grant's Tomb is a U.S. National Monument honoring Ulysses S. Grant. He was a Civil War hero and the eighteenth president of the United States. Grant was born in Ohio and went to West Point for military training. As a young man, he fought in the Mexican War. In the Civil War, he led the North to victory in key battles at Shiloh and Vicksburg. Grant was made general-in-chief of the U.S. armies. He brought the war to a close by defeating Confederate General Robert E. Lee in Virginia. Grant went on to serve two terms as president.

Grant died in 1885. His large funeral included a parade through New York City. That same year the Grant Monument Association (GMA) was formed. Its purpose was to raise money to build a tomb for Grant. Grant's body was placed in a temporary tomb in Riverside Park in Manhattan. Work on the tomb began there six years later. Twelve years after Grant's death, the tomb was dedicated on Grant Day. About one million people came to the ceremony.

The monument is the largest tomb in North America. The building is made of 8,000 tons of granite. It has marble floors and railings, tall white pillars, and a high dome. On the face of the building are the words "Let us have peace." The main room has four statues that tell the story of Grant's life and displays that tell about Grant's career and the building of the tomb. Colorful mosaic tiles show scenes from the Civil War. In the middle of the room are circular railings. From there, one can look into the room below and see the tombs of Grant and his wife, Julia Dent Grant. Two smaller rooms contain maps that show Civil War battle sites.

In the first few years after the tomb was built, more than a half-million people visited it each year. In the 1950s, the GMA passed control of the tomb to the government. By 1990 Grant's Tomb had become an eyesore. Water had cracked the stone, graffiti covered the walls, and the statues were in ruins. A new GMA was formed, and repairs were begun. The tomb was cleaned and restored, and the Park Service keeps watch for vandals. The GMA has plans for a visitors' center behind the tomb. There, people will be able to learn more about Grant and the Civil War.

Reading Time _____

Recalling Facts

1. Ulysses S. Grant was born in
   - ❑ a. Ohio.
   - ❑ b. Mexico.
   - ❑ c. New York.

2. In the Civil War, Grant led the North to win key battles at
   - ❑ a. Toledo and Detroit.
   - ❑ b. Philadelphia and Harrisburg.
   - ❑ c. Shiloh and Vicksburg.

3. The _____ was formed to raise money to build a tomb for Grant.
   - ❑ a. Presidential Tomb Foundation
   - ❑ b. Grant Monument Association
   - ❑ c. Civil War Memorial Service

4. Grant's Tomb is located in
   - ❑ a. New York City.
   - ❑ b. Virginia.
   - ❑ c. Washington, D.C.

5. The tomb is made of
   - ❑ a. brick.
   - ❑ b. granite.
   - ❑ c. wood.

Understanding Ideas

6. Which of the following sentences tells what the whole passage is about?
   - ❑ a. Grant's Tomb honors a Civil War hero and U.S. president.
   - ❑ b. Grant's Tomb is made of 8,000 tons of granite and has marble floors.
   - ❑ c. At Grant's Tomb, visitors can learn about the Civil War.

7. Grant's Tomb
   - ❑ a. was inexpensive to build.
   - ❑ b. was neglected for many years.
   - ❑ c. tells the story of the Civil War from a civilian's point of view.

8. The number of people laid to rest in Grant's Tomb is
   - ❑ a. one.
   - ❑ b. two.
   - ❑ c. three.

9. From the passage, one can infer that Grant
   - ❑ a. died in disgrace.
   - ❑ b. was very popular at the time of his death.
   - ❑ c. did not possess leadership qualities.

10. When visiting Grant's Tomb today, one is least likely to see
    - ❑ a. displays that tell about Grant's career.
    - ❑ b. maps of Civil War battles.
    - ❑ c. broken statues.

The Battle of Vicksburg

A key battle of the Civil War took place in Vicksburg, Mississippi, in 1863. Vicksburg is on the Mississippi River. The river divided the South into two sections. President Abraham Lincoln believed that if the Union troops could take Vicksburg they could control the river, which would break the South in half. In March, General Ulysses S. Grant tried to get Union boats past Vicksburg. His first tries failed. Then Grant came up with a brilliant plan to take the city. In April he marched his men down the west side of the river, below Vicksburg. Admiral David Dixon Porter of the Union fleet ran his boats past the South's guns. The boats brought supplies for the army and carried the troops across the river.

Grant knew he had to defeat the Confederate forces at the city of Jackson before marching on Vicksburg. If not, the Confederate forces could have come up behind him. In May, Grant took control of the city of Jackson. On the way to Vicksburg, Grant's troops fought John C. Pemberton's men. Grant forced Pemberton back to Vicksburg. Grant attacked Vicksburg twice but lost both times. He decided that the only way to take Vicksburg was by siege. Grant cut off Pemberton's supplies and kept firing on the city. On July 4, hunger and disease forced Pemberton to give up. Grant had won.

1. Recognizing Words in Context

Find the word *brilliant* in the passage. One definition below is closest to the meaning of that word. One definition has the opposite or nearly the opposite meaning. The remaining definition has a completely different meaning. Label the definitions C for *closest*, O for *opposite or nearly opposite*, and D for *different*.

_____ a. intelligent and inventive

_____ b. unintelligent and dull

_____ c. stale

2. Distinguishing Fact from Opinion

Two of the statements below present *facts*, which can be proved. The other statement is an *opinion*, which expresses someone's thoughts or beliefs. Label the statements F for *fact* and O for *opinion*.

_____ a. The battle of Vicksburg took place in Mississippi in 1863.

_____ b. Grant was the best commander in the Civil War.

_____ c. Grant decided to take Vicksburg by siege.

3. Keeping Events in Order

Number the statements below 1, 2, and 3 to show the order in which the events took place.

_____ a. On July 4, Pemberton surrendered.

_____ b. On the way to Vicksburg, Grant's troops fought Pemberton's men.

_____ c. Grant thought of a brilliant plan to take Vicksburg.

4. Making Correct Inferences

Two of the statements below are correct *inferences,* or reasonable guesses. They are based on information in the passage. The other statement is an incorrect, or faulty, inference. Label the statements C for *correct* inference and F for *faulty* inference.

_____ a. General Grant was not good at military strategy.

_____ b. General Grant was a creative thinker.

_____ c. The battle of Vicksburg was one of the most important battles of the Civil War.

5. Understanding Main Ideas

One of the statements below expresses the main idea of the passage. One statement is too general, or too broad. The other explains only part of the passage; it is too narrow. Label the statements M for *main idea,* B for *too broad,* and N for *too narrow.*

_____ a. Grant commanded the Union forces.

_____ b. Grant's plan was essential to winning the important and strategic battle of Vicksburg.

_____ c. In May, Grant took control of the city of Jackson.

Correct Answers, Part A _____

Correct Answers, Part B _____

Total Correct Answers _____

ANSWER KEY

READING RATE GRAPH

COMPREHENSION SCORE GRAPH

COMPREHENSION SKILLS PROFILE GRAPH

ANSWER KEY

1A	1. b	2. a	3. b	4. a	5. c	6. b	7. b	8. c	9. b	10. a
1B	1. D, C, O	2. F, O, F	3. 3, 1, 2	4. C, C, F	5. B, M, N					
2A	1. c	2. a	3. b	4. a	5. c	6. c	7. c	8. a	9. a	10. b
2B	1. O, C, D	2. O, F, F	3. 3, 1, 2	4. C, F, C	5. B, M, N					
3A	1. a	2. c	3. a	4. a	5. b	6. a	7. a	8. b	9. a	10. c
3B	1. O, C, D	2. F, F, O	3. 2, 3, 1	4. F, C, C	5. B, M, N					
4A	1. b	2. c	3. a	4. c	5. b	6. a	7. b	8. a	9. a	10. c
4B	1. O, D, C	2. F, F, O	3. 3, 2, 1	4. F, C, C	5. M, B, N					
5A	1. a	2. c	3. b	4. a	5. c	6. a	7. c	8. b	9. b	10. b
5B	1. C, O, D	2. O, F, F	3. 1, 2, 3	4. C, C, F	5. B, M, N					
6A	1. a	2. a	3. c	4. b	5. b	6. b	7. a	8. b	9. c	10. b
6B	1. O, C, D	2. O, F, F	3. 3, 1, 2	4. F, C, C	5. M, N, B					
7A	1. b	2. a	3. c	4. a	5. b	6. a	7. b	8. c	9. a	10. c
7B	1. D, O, C	2. F, O, F	3. 2, 3, 1	4. C, C, F	5. N, M, B					
8A	1. a	2. b	3. a	4. c	5. c	6. b	7. a	8. b	9. b	10. c
8B	1. C, D, O	2. O, F, F	3. 2, 1, 3	4. C, F, C	5. N, B, M					
9A	1. c	2. a	3. b	4. c	5. a	6. a	7. a	8. c	9. b	10. c
9B	1. C, D, O	2. F, F, O	3. 3, 1, 2	4. C, F, C	5. M, N, B					
10A	1. b	2. b	3. a	4. a	5. c	6. c	7. a	8. b	9. c	10. a
10B	1. O, C, D	2. F, F, O	3. 1, 3, 2	4. F, C, C	5. M, N, B					
11A	1. a	2. c	3. a	4. b	5. c	6. b	7. b	8. b	9. a	10. b
11B	1. C, O, D	2. F, F, O	3. 1, 3, 2	4. F, C, C	5. M, N, B					
12A	1. b	2. a	3. a	4. a	5. c	6. b	7. a	8. c	9. b	10. a
12B	1. C, D, O	2. F, F, O	3. 3, 2, 1	4. F, C, C	5. N, B, M					
13A	1. a	2. c	3. a	4. a	5. b	6. a	7. b	8. c	9. a	10. b
13B	1. O, C, D	2. F, O, F	3. 1, 2, 3	4. C, C, F	5. M, B, N					

14A	1. b	2. a	3. b	4. c	5. a	6. b	7. a	8. b	9. b	10. c
14B	1. D, C, O	2. F, F, O	3. 3, 1, 2	4. C, C, F	5. N, M, B					
15A	1. a	2. b	3. c	4. b	5. a	6. b	7. a	8. c	9. b	10. c
15B	1. O, C, D	2. O, F, F	3. 2, 3, 1	4. F, C, C	5. M, N, B					
16A	1. c	2. a	3. b	4. a	5. a	6. a	7. c	8. c	9. a	10. b
16B	1. C, O, D	2. O, F, F	3. 1, 3, 2	4. C, C, F	5. M, N, B					
17A	1. c	2. b	3. c	4. b	5. a	6. a	7. b	8. b	9. b	10. c
17B	1. C, O, D	2. F, O, F	3. 2, 1, 3	4. C, C, F	5. M, N, B					
18A	1. a	2. c	3. b	4. c	5. b	6. b	7. a	8. a	9. c	10. b
18B	1. D, C, O	2. F, O, F	3. 3, 1, 2	4. C, C, F	5. M, B, N					
19A	1. c	2. a	3. b	4. a	5. b	6. c	7. b	8. b	9. a	10. c
19B	1. D, O, C	2. F, F, O	3. 2, 1, 3	4. C, C, F	5. M, B, N					
20A	1. c	2. a	3. b	4. a	5. c	6. a	7. c	8. b	9. b	10. a
20B	1. C, D, O	2. F, F, O	3. 2, 3, 1	4. C, C, F	5. B, N, M					
21A	1. b	2. b	3. c	4. c	5. a	6. b	7. c	8. b	9. a	10. c
21B	1. O, C, D	2. F, O, F	3. 2, 3, 1	4. C, F, C	5. N, M, B					
22A	1. b	2. a	3. c	4. a	5. b	6. b	7. a	8. c	9. a	10. b
22B	1. O, C, D	2. F, F, O	3. 3, 2, 1	4. C, C, F	5. M, B, N					
23A	1. a	2. c	3. b	4. a	5. b	6. c	7. a	8. b	9. a	10. b
23B	1. O, C, D	2. F, F, O	3. 1, 2, 3	4. C, F, C	5. M, N, B					
24A	1. c	2. a	3. a	4. b	5. b	6. c	7. c	8. c	9. b	10. a
24B	1. C, O, D	2. O, F, F	3. 1, 3, 2	4. C, C, F	5. M, B, N					
25A	1. a	2. c	3. b	4. a	5. b	6. a	7. b	8. b	9. b	10. c
25B	1. C, O, D	2. F, O, F	3. 3, 2, 1	4. F, C, C	5. B, M, N					

Reading Rate

Put an X on the line above each lesson number to show your reading time and words-per-minute rate for that lesson.

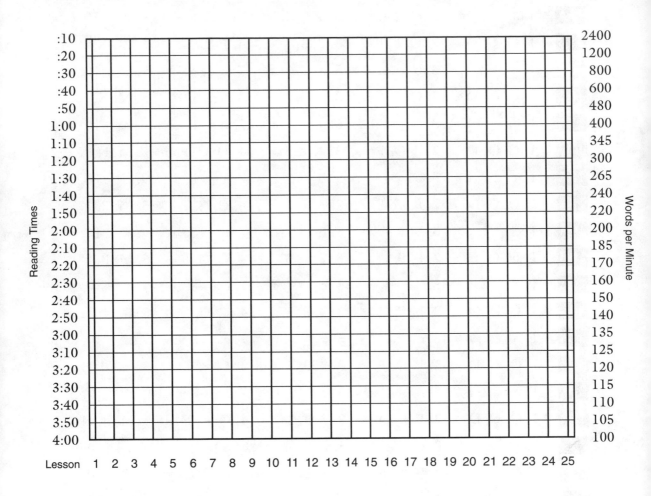

COMPREHENSION SCORE

Put an X on the line above each lesson number to indicate your total correct answers and comprehension score for that lesson.

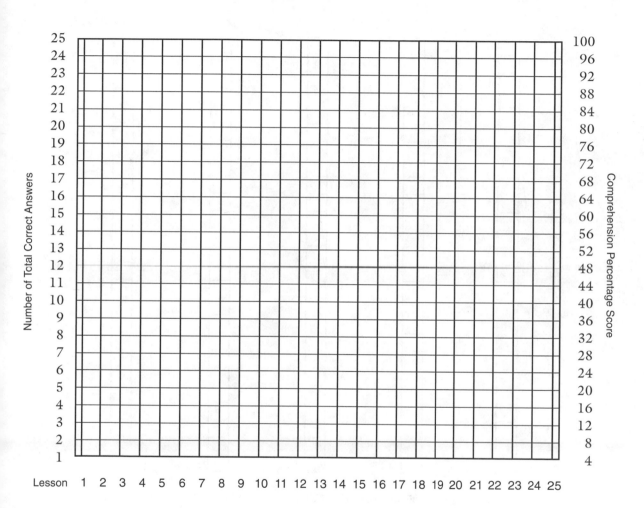

COMPREHENSION SKILLS PROFILE

Put an X in the box above each question type to indicate an incorrect reponse to any part of that question.

	Recognizing Words in Context	Distinguishing Fact from Opinion	Keeping Events in Order	Making Correct Inferences	Understanding Main Ideas
Lesson 1					
2					
3					
4					
5					
6					
7					
8					
9					
10					
11					
12					
13					
14					
15					
16					
17					
18					
19					
20					
21					
22					
23					
24					
25					